I Love God's Green Earth

Devotions for Kids Who Want to
Take Care of God's CREATION

Michael & Caroline
CARROLL

Tyndale House Publishers, Inc.
Carol Stream, Illinois

Visit Tyndale's exciting Web site for kids at www.tyndale.com/kids.

TYNDALE is a registered trademark of Tyndale House Publishers, Inc.

Tyndale Kids logo is a trademark of Tyndale House Publishers, Inc.

I Love God's Green Earth: Devotions for Kids Who Want to Take Care of God's Creation

Designed by Jennifer Ghionzoli

Edited by Stephanie Voiland

Published in association with the literary agency of WordServe Literary Group, Ltd., 10152 S. Knoll Circle, Highlands Ranch, CO 80130.

For manufacturing information regarding this product, please call 1-800-323-9400.

Library of Congress Cataloging-in-Publication Data

Carroll, Michael W., date.
  I love God's green earth : devotions for kids who want to take care of God's creation / Michael and Caroline Carroll.
    p. cm.
  "Tyndale kids."
  ISBN 978-1-4143-3179-9 (sc)
  1. Human ecology—Religious aspects—Christianity—Juvenile literature.
2. Christian children—Prayers and devotions. I. Carroll, Caroline, date. II. Title.
  BT695.5.C373 2010
  261.8'8—dc22   2009042428

Printed in the United States of America

16 15 14 13 12 11 10
 7   6   5   4   3   2   1

To Harriet & Arne Truman,
the original repair/reuse/recycle/reduce organic gardeners

Contents

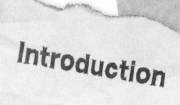

Sing a new song to the LORD! Let the whole earth sing
to the LORD! . . . Let the heavens be glad, and the earth
rejoice! Let the sea and everything in it shout his praise!
Let the fields and their crops burst out with joy! Let the
trees of the forest rustle with praise before the LORD!
PSALM 96:1, 11-13

PSALM 96 TELLS US that God created a world of
celebration. He wants us to live a life of joy. Part of our
joy here on Earth comes from spending time outdoors in
the beauty of the world he made. Many people in the Bible
went out into the deserts, hills, and mountains so they
could get away from distractions and connect with God.
John the Baptist, David, many of the Old Testament proph-
ets, and even Jesus went to wild and quiet places to talk
with God. Spending time in nature brought them closer
to him. They kept their lives in balance by being in touch
with God and his creation.

The Garden of Eden was created in perfect balance, and
Adam and Eve were there to take care of it. But Adam and
Eve chose not to follow God's instructions, so God sent
them out of his Garden and into a world filled with
thorns, weeds, droughts, and storms. Even though
we live outside of the Garden now, God still provides a beautiful world for us and wants us to
take care of it.

People haven't always done a good job of this.
Carbon monoxide pumps into the sky, garbage
fills up the land, and chemicals pour into the
rivers. Some scientists say global warming—
a rise of temperatures all over the world—
will create massive droughts and cause

food to run low. Are these scientists right? And should we be scared, or should we be excited to help change things? The fact is, scary news is not the reason we should care for the world. We should take care of the Earth because that's our job, because we love others, and because it makes God happy.

Joy comes when life is in balance. But some parts of our world are out of balance. In this book, we'll find ways to help bring balance to God's creation. As we do, we'll understand more about God's design for the universe, and we'll learn about our role in his plan for Earth.

EACH DEVOTION INCLUDES:

Scripture: A verse or passage that reflects God's love and care for his world or describes the part you can play in "creation care."

Facts: A section on the scientific facts surrounding the day's topic.

Connection: This section links the scientific facts with the biblical truth from that day's Scripture passage.

What Can I Do?: Each devotion will include an action you can take, which may include tips on how to **reuse** stuff, **recycle** stuff, **reduce** the amount of stuff you use, **rethink** the way you use stuff, **respect** God's world, **reflect** on new ideas, or **relay** your thoughts to God.

Fun Stuff: jokes, riddles, or factoids that tie in with the theme of the day.

In learning these things, we'll get closer to our Creator. Now *that's* cause for celebration!

We want to hear from you. If this book gives you any cool thoughts or ideas about how you can take care of God's world, please send us an e-mail and tell us about it. We will write you back.

Our e-mail address is
cosmicart@stock-space-images.com.

What Started All the Chaos

DAY 1

The LORD God called to [Adam], "Where are you?"
GENESIS 3:9

THINGS WERE PRETTY peachy in the Garden of Eden. Adam and Eve had the best salad bar in history, and they lived in peace with God's creatures and his creation. Everything worked just right together. God asked only one thing of the first humans: don't eat fruit from this one tree. Guess what? They did. When Adam and Eve disobeyed, everything stopped working together. Four things happened:

1. Humans were separated from God.
2. Humans were separated from each other, and they began to disagree and argue.
3. Every human was separated from himself or herself. People no longer felt good about themselves (Adam and Eve were ashamed). They were confused about their own thoughts and feelings.
4. Humans were separated from God's creation. They no longer lived in peace with it.

Then God did an amazing thing. He sent his Son, Jesus, to build a bridge between himself and us. Even though our sin has separated us from God, Jesus died so that we could reconnect with God. When we follow Jesus and let him be in charge of our lives, God's bridge reaches all the way from him to us.

2

Connection

In the Garden of Eden, Adam and Eve were without shame until they sinned and stopped following God's plan. Then Adam was so ashamed that when God came to see him, as he did every day, Adam hid (see Genesis 3). Adam was no longer close to God. Jesus provides a way for us to get close to God, and as we learn more about God and get closer to him, we become more like Jesus. Love becomes the way we operate in life as the separation between humans and God (#1 on the list) is mended. This doesn't happen all at once; it's a lifelong journey that begins to heal the separation of humans from each other and from themselves (#2 and #3). The last separation, between God's creation and us, is what this book is all about. Like with #2 and #3, the healing of this one takes time. But with God's help, we can reconnect not only with him but also with his creation.

What Can I Do?

Relay *your thoughts to God.* We stay close to God by talking with him and listening to him. He speaks to us through his Word. Sometimes he shows us the way through events and circumstances that happen to us. Stay close to God, and he will help you make wise decisions about his garden, the world.

Garden Grins

Q: Why do potatoes make good detectives?
A: Because they keep their eyes peeled.

Q: What vegetable do you need a plumber for?
A: A leek.

3

Made in God's Image

God created human beings in his own image.
In the image of God he created them.
GENESIS 1:27

WE ARE MADE in God's image. That means that we have free will and that we have the ability to make choices. He has given us the ability to know what is right and what is wrong. We can live a life that reminds people of God by showing others love, patience, and kindness.

Knowing that we're made in God's image, how should we live? How should we treat his world? Let's think about God's qualities as they relate to his creation:

God creates; he does not destroy.
God cares for the weak.
God rescues the helpless.
God renews instead of "using up."
God brings beautiful order, not disorder.
God restores the damaged and broken.

Here are some names of God found in the Bible: the Shield, the Healer, the Gardener, my Helper, my Song, my Source, the Spring of Living Water, our Resting Place. These names of God show us that he wants the best for us and the rest of his creation, and that he protects and loves us.

 Connection

As we learn in the first chapter of Genesis, Creation is designed for us to enjoy and care for, working hand in hand with God. He has desired a relationship with us ever since the beginning of the world. He's saying, "Work with me, people!"

What Can I Do?

Reflect on who God is. Think of some of the things you appreciate most about God, such as his patience with you, his willingness to forgive you, or his constant love. Ask him to make you more like him in those areas.

Amazing Facts:

* No one knows for sure how many different kinds of creatures God has created, but there are 1.5 to 1.8 million different kinds that have been named. Each species, or kind, has its own unique characteristics. About half of all species are insects.

* There are more than 300,000 different species of beetles.

* There are about 4,500 species of mammals. Scientists have found more than 400 new species of mammals over the past 15 years.

To Serve and Protect

May the LORD bless you and protect you.
NUMBERS 6:24

HAVE YOU EVER noticed the words on the side of a police car? In many cities, the door of a patrol car says, "To Serve and Protect." Genesis 2:15 says the Lord put people in the Garden of Eden to "tend and watch over it" (NLT) or to "work it and take care of it" (NIV). The original Bible words (in Hebrew) are *abad* and *shamar*, which actually mean to "serve and protect." Many law enforcement people don't realize their patrol cars are quoting the last part of a Bible verse!

Part of serving God is taking care of the "garden" he has given us to live in—the world around us. We can take care of his creation by being careful of where we put our garbage, how we use our water, and how we make and use energy. But what's this bit about protecting? God also calls us to care for his creatures and their homes, to preserve clean water and air, and to not use up all the wilderness. Is the whole Earth too big to protect? Is it too late? There are things that all of us can do to be better Earth keepers. A lot of people think the problems are too big. They say, "What can *I* do? I'm just one person." But God has used a lot of "just one persons" to do some amazing things.

Connection

As we see in Genesis 2, "The LORD God placed the man in the
Garden of Eden to tend and watch over it." That is one reason God
has put us here: to watch and tend his "garden," the world. Each of
us can do our part to care for creation, and when we work together,
big things can happen! An African proverb says, "Many little
people in many little places doing many little things can change the
world." A multitude of people just changing the way they do one or
two things can have a major impact. So you don't have to do huge
things. Believe this: with God's help, every little bit that you do
makes a difference.

What Can I Do?

Respect the land. Make a game of picking up one piece of trash
every time you are outside. One of the best ways to protect the
land and water is simply to clean up! Trash not only clogs rivers
and makes wildlife sick but it also takes away from God's beauty
around us.

Joke

Q: What promise did Adam and Eve make after they were
kicked out of the Garden of Eden?

A: They promised to turn over a new leaf.

The Starfish

I tell you the truth, whatever you did **for one of the**
least of these . . . you did **for me.**
MATTHEW 25:40, NIV

THERE'S A STORY about a little boy at the seashore. As he
walked along the sand, he noticed hundreds of starfish that
had been washed high up onto the beach the night before by
a fierce storm. He knew they would never make it back to the
water on their own, so he started picking them up one by one
and carrying them back to the water so they would live. His older
brother came along and said, "That's stupid. Why are you even
bothering to do that? There are so many of them, it's not going to
make any difference." The little boy looked down at the starfish
in his hand, dropped it into the water, and said, "Well, it makes a
difference to that one."

Even little kids can do things to help take care of God's
world. The boy carrying the starfish back to the water
was doing what he could to help some of God's creatures who were in trouble.

 Connection

In Matthew 25:40, Jesus was talking about taking care of other people who need our help. But fish, birds, and animals—even the Earth itself—need our help too, as we learned in Genesis 1:26. Are you going to do every single thing that we mention in this book to help the planet? Of course not. But even if you only do *one* thing, it will make a difference.

 What Can I Do?

Relay your thoughts to God. "Lord, there are 6 billion people on this Earth, and I am just one of them. Please show me what you want me to do to make your world a little better. Thank you."

Joke

Q: What fish always gets asked for his autograph?

A: The starfish.

The Real Creator

Turn from these worthless things and turn to the living God, who made heaven and earth, the sea, and everything in them.
ACTS 14:15

THE WORLD IS full of ideas about God. Some are right; others are not. Some people have the mistaken idea that God created the world but then took a vacation. In other words, they think God made the universe to be like a giant machine and then sat back to watch it run down like an old clock. People who believe this think that God is not interested in what happens here on Earth. But that is not true. Genesis tells us that at the end of the creation week, God looked at all he had made "and he saw that it was very good!" (Genesis 1:31). He put his stamp of approval on the whole universe; he is very interested in what happens to it!

Another wrong idea is that God and creation are the same thing. Some people think that God is in the trees and flowers and creatures and air. But Genesis, the first book in the Bible, tells us that God existed even before the world was made and that he is separate from it. God tells us not to worship anyone or anything besides him. And that includes nature.

God is better than all those ideas. He's greater, bigger, more awesome and amazing than his creation, but he also cares about the world he has created.

 ## Connection

When some people do things for the environment, it is because they love the Earth. This isn't a bad thing, but it's not the whole story. When Christians take care of God's creation, we have an extra good reason: we do it out of love for our Father in heaven—the one "who made heaven and earth"!

 ## What Can I Do?

Reflect on who God is. We can make sure we have a clear view of who God is by studying his Word, the Bible. We can trust the Bible to be true because it is "God-breathed" (2 Timothy 3:16, NIV). That means the words in it are just what God wants to tell us. So if we hear something about God, we should always check in with what the Bible says about it.

 ## A Child's Prayer

A mother overheard this bedtime prayer by her little boy: "Dear God, please take care of my daddy and mommy and me. Oh, and please take care of yourself, God. If anything happens to you, we're going to be in a big mess."

DAY 6 What Do You Love?

Jesus said, "Simon son of John, do you truly love me?"
He answered, "Yes, Lord, you know that I love you."
Jesus said, "Take care of my sheep."
JOHN 21:16, NIV

HANNA LOVES MUSIC. There is one band that is her absolute
favorite, though. She *loves* their music. She listens to it all the
time. She goes to the band's concerts whenever she can. She owns
all their music, and she collects their posters and T-shirts.

Hanna takes good care of her music, posters, and T-shirts
because they have something to do with the band she loves. She
knows the band puts a lot of work into their songs, and Hanna
honors her favorite band by taking care of what they have made.

God is the *great* musician. The song of his creation drifts on the
winds, thunders in the clouds, and lilts in the voices of birds and
bugs. He's not distant from what he has made. God created and
is redeeming this world, and he is healing it through the power of
Jesus. He cares for our planet. If we love God, we'll care for it too.
If you love the Creator, care for his creation. It's just that simple.

12

 ## Connection

In today's verse, Jesus tells Simon Peter that if he truly loves Jesus, he will take care of Jesus' "sheep." Jesus' sheep are his followers. If we truly love God, we will take care of his family, his creatures, and his world.

What Can I Do?

Respect *God's world.* One way we can show God how much we love him is to care for the things he loves, whether that's people or other parts of his creation. Even when we feel frustrated with a friend or family member, Jesus wants us to treat that person like a treasure, with care and love.

Fun Fact

One of the most common musical instruments mentioned in the Bible is the lyre. It had eight or ten strings and a sound box, much like a guitar today. Lyres that are 4,750 years old have been found in the ancient city of Ur.

Joke

Son: Mom, I want to grow up and be a rock 'n' roll musician.
Mom: Well, Son, you've got to pick one or the other. You can't do both.

Love One Another

Respect everyone, and love your Christian
brothers and sisters.
1 PETER 2:17

IT MIGHT SEEM kind of strange to think about loving people who haven't even been born yet, but it's important. In the Scripture above, Peter tells us to love our Christian brothers and sisters. Jesus tells us to love our neighbors, and in a way, the people who come after us are our future "neighbors." Until Jesus comes back, future generations of people are going to live on this planet—maybe even your own children and grandchildren someday. Did you know there are things you can do now that will show either love or disrespect to these people in the future?

As our world's population grows, we need to be more and more careful about how we use the resources God gives us. God has given us an entire planet filled with rich soil for plants, clean water, sunshine, and clear air. We don't want to leave future generations a polluted world full of trash. We can love and respect others by leaving them a clean and healthy world.

 ## Connection

Jesus said, "Do to others as you would like them to do to you" (Luke 6:31). This includes leaving their future home—the Earth—the way we would want it to be.

 ## What Can I Do?

Respect the Earth. The good care we take of our Earth shows our love for God and for the people of the future. But don't be preachy or bossy to others about taking care of God's Earth. Nobody likes to be nagged. Just lead by your example: Pick up some trash, even if it's not yours. Bring your lunch to school in a reusable bag. Be creative! You'll be surprised to see what good things happen.

 ## Crazy Fact

There are 6.77 billion people on Earth. If things continue as they have been, there will be 9 billion people on Earth by 2040.

DAY 8

How Big Is Your Footprint?

Guide my steps by your word,
so I will not be overcome by evil.
PSALM 119:133

WHAT'S AN ECOLOGICAL FOOTPRINT? It's a measurement of the energy, air, water, and soil you use. It is based on the things you do and the way you live. Your ecological footprint is based on a combination of lots of things: how far you ride in a car each day; how much water you use when you shower, brush your teeth, and use the toilet; the foods you eat; the clothes you wear; and the vacations you take. So . . . the smaller your footprint, the better for the Earth.

Bigfoot Jokes

Q: Why didn't the runner agree to race Bigfoot?
A: He couldn't stand de-feet.

Q: What do you get when you cross Bigfoot with a kangaroo?
A: A fur coat with big pockets.

Q: What steps should you take if you see Bigfoot in the forest?
A: Very large ones.

Connection

God helps us do right in every part of our lives, including making wise choices about how we treat our Earth. The point of this book is not to make you feel guilty or bad about the things you do and the way you live, but to help you think about the everyday choices you make in a new way. As the Bible says, "What counts is whether we have been transformed into a new creation" (Galatians 6:15).

What Can I Do?

Rethink *your choices.* One way you can change is to start making choices that are gentler on our Earth. There are several good sites to help you figure out how big your ecological footprint is. Go to http://www.islandwood.org/kids/impact/footprint/footprint.php and discover *your* impact on our world. Are you an ecological Bigfoot?

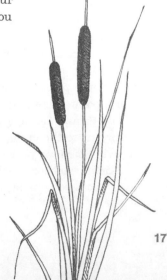

Get Connected:
A Chat with a Professor

Who let the wild donkey go free? . . .
I gave him the wasteland as his home, the salt flats
as his habitat. He laughs at the commotion in the town;
he does not hear a driver's shout. He ranges the hills for his pasture
and searches for any green thing.
JOB 39:5-8, NIV

WHAT DO YOU see when you look through your bedroom
window? Buildings and lights? What do you hear? Cars and
other street noise? These man-made things are not bad in themselves, but sometimes they give people a wrong view of their own
importance. They begin to think they are the makers of everything.
That's one reason God's creation is so important. Professor Steven
Bouma-Prediger of Hope College puts it this way: "When we're
struck by the beauty and the glory of the natural world, we realize
our proper place, which is *not* at the center of things."

He points out that people usually think of creation care as giving up things. He says people often view it as "a life of sacrifice." But
according to the professor, "It's also putting up a bird feeder and
drawing birds to your backyard. It's going outside. It's bicycling. It's
walking." In other words, taking care of God's Earth doesn't take
away from your life; it adds to it.

Connection

The donkey God is talking about in today's passage is happy living in God's creation. It enjoys the world as a gift from God. How can we be good creation "caregivers"? It starts with a closer walk with the Creator. We can do this through praying to him, having friendships with other Christians, and reading his Word. But there is also another way. Being in tune with God's creation helps us to be in tune with God. Get connected with him! Like Job's donkey, appreciate the works of God's hands.

What Can I Do?

Reconnect *with nature.* Put up that bird feeder. Go for a walk. Enjoy the sunlight and creatures and wind and trees. Make every outdoor exploration a prayer of thanks to the God who loves you and loves his creation!

Reflect *on the outdoors.* In *The Diary of a Young Girl*, Anne Frank writes about being locked in an attic, hiding from the Nazis during World War II. She says, "The best remedy for those who are afraid, lonely or unhappy is to go outside, somewhere where they can be quiet, alone with the heavens, nature and God. Because only then does one feel that all is as it should be and that God wishes to see people happy, amidst the simple beauty of nature."

Some Bright News

Getting out in the sun for just a few minutes each day can help prevent many kinds of diseases. It gives us a natural form of vitamin D.

19

Renewing from the Ground Up:

DAY 10 How God Recycles the Rocks

Every valley shall be raised up,
every mountain and hill made low.
ISAIAH 40:4, NIV

MANY PEOPLE LIKE to think that the concept of recycling was invented by humans. But actually God came up with the idea in the first place—he designed our planet to renew itself, and the Earth has been doing the recycling thing for a long time.

The Earth is like a gigantic recycling machine. Its air, water, and minerals all recycle themselves to provide a safe, healthy environment for God's creatures. The unique design of Earth's recycling systems is one of the ways our world is different from any other planet. It was created just right for life.

One of God's recycling plans involves the ground we stand on. If the rock and soil on Earth weren't renewed, all the minerals would wash away from the mountains and land and end up at the bottom of the ocean. Meanwhile, our soil would die, plants wouldn't grow, and things would just be a mess. But the Earth gives itself a face-lift by a process called plate tectonics.

Here's how it works: The thin crust of the Earth is split into big sections, called plates. These plates move around, sometimes so slowly you can't feel them, and sometimes all at once, like when an earthquake strikes. Some bump into each other, raising mountain chains and causing earthquakes. Others slip under each other,

where the rock melts under great heat and pressure. Thanks to all that moving and shaking, minerals that wash down onto the ocean floor from the land don't just sit there. They slip back into Earth's hot interior. There, they are recycled, pushing back out as new mountains or as molten rock from volcanoes. Either way, God's planetary "conveyor belt" renews the land.

Connection

It takes heat and pressure to make rocks into something good. In Zechariah 13:9, God tells his people that he will bring them "through the fire and make them pure. I will refine them like silver and purify them like gold. They will call on my name, and I will answer them." Is there something in your life that feels like fiery heat? like pressure? How do you think God is using those forces to make something good in your life? Always remember that he is bringing you to a closer place with him.

What Can I Do?

Relay your thoughts to God. "Lord, thank you for the power beneath our feet and for bringing life to all things by recycling rock plates. I see your power in the mountains and volcanoes that make new soil, and I see your power in the way you renew me, too."

Fun Fact

The Earth's plates move about as quickly as your fingernails grow.

Exploding Recyclers

You came near and stood at the foot of the mountain, while
flames from the mountain shot into the sky. The mountain was
shrouded in black clouds and deep darkness.

DEUTERONOMY 4:11

WHEN GOD GAVE Moses the Ten Commandments on Mount
Sinai, the flaming mountain was "shrouded in black clouds
and deep darkness." Volcanoes remind us of how Moses must have
felt on that special day. Volcanoes are mountains that blow their
tops. Some of them, called shield volcanoes, have gently sloping
sides and lava that erupts slowly. The beautiful Hawaiian Islands
are shield volcanoes. Other volcanoes, called stratovolcanoes, are far
more dangerous. They explode thousands of feet into the sky. Their
molten rock and ash blow across many miles, burning forests and
buildings and burying them under a layer of volcanic ash.

Believe it or not, within all this violence something good is happening. Minerals pour out from deep within the Earth, making
fresh, rich soil that will help new crops and trees grow. And something else happens: volcanoes recycle the air. Rocks in the ground
react with the atmosphere so that parts of our air get pulled into
the minerals in the rocks.

Do you want to know what Earth would look like if it weren't
for our volcanoes? Take a peek at Mars. The red rocks of Mars
are essentially rusted: the oxygen in the air is now trapped in the
stones. Here on Earth, gases from our atmosphere get locked in rock
too, but that rock melts beneath the plates. In volcanic eruptions, the

gases are freed and come out into the air again.
Because of volcanoes, we have not only new minerals in the
ground, but also fresh air!

 Connection

The rocks on Mars are tinted red because they have soaked up
the oxygen around them. The Spirit of God is around us, too. As
we soak it up by being with him in prayer, reading the Bible, and
spending time with other Christians, we take on a joyful "tint." God
wants you to reflect his joy. In Romans 15:13 Paul says, "I pray that
God, the source of hope, will fill you completely with joy and peace
because you trust in him. Then you will overflow with confident
hope through the power of the Holy Spirit."

 What Can I Do?

Reflect *on the power of God's creation.* What
forces of nature are the most awesome to you?
How do these forces make life on Earth better?

 Amazing Fact

Volcanoes can be destructive, but God has given
us minds and wisdom to learn how to predict eruptions so we can
stay out of their way. One such eruption was the stratovolcano
Mount Pinatubo in the Philippines. Its most recent eruption was in
1991. Thanks to scientists' warnings, 60,000 people moved to safety
before the volcano erupted.

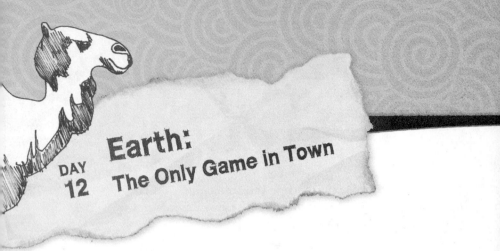

Earth:
The Only Game in Town

Trust in the LORD always,
for the LORD GOD is the eternal Rock.
ISAIAH 26:4

THERE ARE OTHER planets that have a stony crust like Earth. Mercury, Venus, and Mars are called terrestrial, or "earthlike," worlds, because they have solid, rocky surfaces and thin atmospheres. These planets have volcanoes, too, but those volcanoes no longer recycle air and minerals. The reason? None of the other planets have plate tectonics, as we talked about on day #10. Even if those planets had cool rain showers and nice air to breathe (they don't), their minerals just lie on the ground with nothing to renew them. None of them can support the kind of life found here in our own home world. Earth is a one-of-a-kind planet.

 Connection

Knowing a little bit about how God designed the Earth and its rocks helps us appreciate the great Designer and his plans for us. In fact, he used the image of a rock to give us an idea of what he is like. The Bible calls God "the Rock of our salvation" (Psalm 95:1). God is even more solid than the rocks beneath our feet. He never shifts or changes.

 What Can I Do?

Reflect on God's design. God's world does not simply run automatically, for no reason, or by accident. It is crafted so that plants and animals, and you and I, can live here. So the next time you feel the Earth tremble under your feet, hear about a volcano, or even see a plant growing out of fine soil, remember who the real Rock is. He loves Earth, which he has designed with beauty and balance, and he cares for you even more!

Relay your thoughts to God. "Lord, when life is hard, help me to remember that you are my Rock, a strong place to put my feet, a firm wall to lean against when I feel weak. Thank you for always being there, even in those times when I forget about you."

 Crazy Fact

As you read these words, some 600 volcanoes are ready to erupt—or actually erupting—around the world. Many are under the ocean!

 Cool Fact

Republican president Theodore Roosevelt (1901-1909) established more than 100 national forests and almost two dozen wildlife refuges and national monuments. One of those monuments was the incredible display of rocks called the Grand Canyon.

25

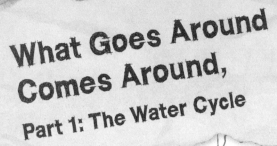

What Goes Around Comes Around,

Part 1: The Water Cycle

> The rain and snow come down from the heavens and stay
> on the ground to water the earth. They cause the grain to grow,
> producing seed for the farmer and bread for the hungry.
> ISAIAH 55:10

ONE OF THE Earth's most important recycling systems is the water cycle. Rain and snow come down from the sky, watering plants and filling oceans, lakes, and rivers. Water flows down from the mountains into the lakes and seas, where it evaporates (turns into gas form, or vapor) and goes back into the air. Up in the sky, the water vapor gathers into clouds, eventually coming back down again as rain or snow. And around and around the cycle goes.

The really cool thing about the water cycle is that when water turns to vapor, no matter how dirty the water is, it leaves behind all the dirt and goes back into the air clean and purified. Even seawater, which has lots of salt in it, goes back into the air as pure, fresh water. It's the perfect purification system, built right into our environment.

Connection

Isaiah 30:23, 25 shows a picture of God taking care of his people: "The LORD will bless you with rain at planting time. . . . There will be streams of water flowing down every mountain and hill." God's plan for recycling water is one way he takes care of us.

What Can I Do?

Relay your thoughts to God. "Lord, sometimes I feel dirty. I feel like

things I've done or thoughts I've had stick to me like mud. But just like water is purified in the evaporating process, I know you can make me clean. Thank you for forgiving me for the things I have done that are not clean. Help me to love the things that you love."

Rethink *what goes into the water.* God uses the water cycle to keep the world clean, but you can help rivers, lakes, and oceans stay clean too. Don't dump pop, dirty water, or paint into rivers or streams, and keep trash out of waterways.

 ## Surprising Fact

The Earth has a limited amount of water. That water keeps being recycled through the water cycle so it stays clean. This means that you may be taking a bath with a molecule or two used to bathe in by a dinosaur, Moses, Queen Esther, and lots of others.

 ## H$_2$O Factoid

Seven-tenths of the Earth is covered with water, but most of it is salty ocean. If you could put all the Earth's water into 100 swimming pools, less than one pool would have drinkable water.

Ocean Jokes

Q: What kind of a phone does the ocean have?
A: A shell phone.

Q: Where did the seaweed find a job?
A: In the "kelp wanted" ads.

Q: What washes up on very small beaches?
A: Microwaves.

27

What Goes Around Comes Around,

DAY 14 Part 2: The Oxygen Cycle

> When you give them your breath, life is created,
> and you renew the face of the earth.
> **PSALM 104:30**

GOD IS SO SMART—think about this recycling plan he invented! He created people and animals to breathe oxygen. The waste product of oxygen that we breathe *out* is called carbon dioxide. So he made plants to breathe *in* carbon dioxide and to breathe *out* oxygen as their waste product. Green plants use the power of sunlight to combine carbon dioxide with water to make sugar and oxygen. The leaves of plants and trees have tiny pores called stomata. Carbon dioxide enters and oxygen leaves through these pores. It's such a cool plan—nothing goes to waste. The air we breathe today is the same air that was breathed by people in Jesus' time—it's just been through the "air recycling" process a bunch of times.

God's world is tied together. People and animals get food and oxygen from plants. Plants get food (fertilizer and minerals) and carbon dioxide from people and animals. It's one of our Creator's perfect balances.

Connection

Lamentations 3:22-23 says, "The faithful love of the LORD never ends! His mercies never cease. Great is his faithfulness; his mercies begin afresh each morning." Just as oxygen is recycled, so is God's faithfulness. It's like a breath of pure, clean air, and it's fresh every day.

What Can I Do?

Reflect *on God's wisdom.* Take a "plant walk" around your neighborhood, and look at the trees, flowers, and plants. As you do, thank God for his great idea of oxygen recycling!

Fun Fact

An average houseplant with 30 leaves breathes out 360 milliliters of oxygen—about the amount in a birthday balloon—in a day. It would take between 300 and 400 plants this size to make one hour's worth of oxygen for a person.

What Goes Around Comes Around,

DAY 15 Part 3: The Soil Cycle

> Other seeds fell on fertile soil, and they sprouted,
> grew, and produced a crop that was thirty, sixty, and even
> a hundred times as much as had been planted!
> MARK 4:8

RECIPE FOR SOIL: Take some rocks, ground up fine. Add minerals, air, water, and humus (black material that was once plants and animals but is now decomposed). Mix well, and voilà! You've got soil. Plants use soil as a source of food and energy as they grow. Eventually the plants die or are gobbled up by animals and bugs. Animal and bug poop turns into soil very quickly. When animals and bugs die, they also turn into soil. Then the cycle starts all over again. Earthworms are a big help in this process too. They are God's little dirt machines, loosening and mixing up the soil so that materials get blended in and plants can spread their roots.

You would think that it would be hard to mess up dirt since the process is so well designed, but our soil has a problem: trash. Here in the United States, each person, on average, throws away his or her own body weight in trash every month. This trash goes into dumps and landfills. A lot of man-made trash, like plastic milk jugs and pop cans, can't be broken down to join the soil cycle. And rotting trash makes a gas called methane, a poisonous gas.

 Connection

God designed soil to nourish plants. When trash gets in the way, plants can't get to the good nutrients in the dirt. As the parable in Mark 4 talks about, God has designed our souls to be nourished

too. He teaches us through circumstances, through his Word, and through wise friends and mentors. But when we put a lot of garbage in (such as watching inappropriate movies or TV shows, or hanging out with the wrong friends), that garbage gets in the way of God's nourishing Spirit. Pretty soon that garbage comes out again as bad habits, nasty language, or simple unhappiness. As they say, garbage in, garbage out. Put another way: God in, God out! What kinds of things are you growing these days?

 ## What Can I Do?

Respect *and recycle.* When you see a piece of trash, pick it up and throw it in the nearest garbage can. If it can be recycled, find a recycling bin to put it in. If you throw away just one piece of trash a day, you're cleaning up three big garbage bags of litter per year!

 ## Cool Fact

There are more individual living organisms in a teaspoon of soil than there are people on Earth.

Soil Jokes

Q: What is dirt?
A: Mud with the juice squeezed out.

Q: How do you know which end of a worm is the head?
A: Tickle the middle and see which end laughs.

The Seasons

You made the moon to mark the seasons,
and the sun knows when to set.
PSALM 104:19

THE EARTH NEEDS time to rest and reboot. God designed the seasons to provide a natural rest for planet Earth. In the sunny summer, plants and trees work hard, growing taller and sprouting new leaves. At the same time, they are pouring out oxygen, freshening the air.

Chlorophyll is the green material that leaves use to trap the energy of sunlight, making food for the plant. As the days grow shorter in the fall, plant growth slows down, and leaves drop to the ground. The dead leaves bring nutrients to the ground as they turn into soil. During the cold winter months when there isn't as much sunlight, many trees and plants become dormant, or rest, until spring. Then the cycle begins again.

 **Connection**

Psalm 104 talks about the seasons God made for the earth. Did you know that our lives are like seasons too? Sometimes we go through times that seem cold and dark—times we feel sad or alone. Other times God brings warmth and new life. The trick is to hold on to God's promises in the difficult winter seasons and celebrate life when the happiness of summer comes again.

 What Can I Do?

Recycle *leaves.* Instead of raking up all those autumn leaves, ask your parents if they can use the lawn mower to mulch the leaves into tiny bits. The leaf bits will turn back into the soil, giving it more nutrients in the spring when the grass comes back.

 Surprising Fact

Leaves don't actually "change color" in autumn. The yellows, reds, and oranges have always been there, hidden by the green chlorophyll. As the green drains away in the fall, the other colors become visible!

Joke

> **Q: If April showers bring May flowers, what do May flowers bring?**
>
> **A: Pilgrims.**

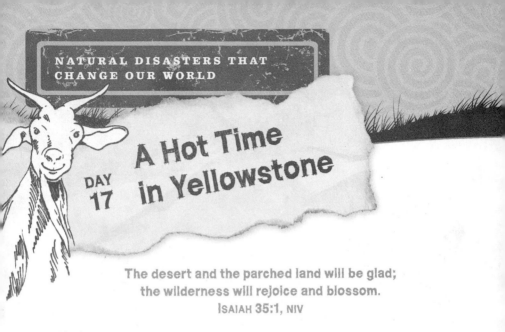

A Hot Time in Yellowstone

DAY 17

The desert and the parched land will be glad;
the wilderness will rejoice and blossom.
ISAIAH 35:1, NIV

YELLOWSTONE NATIONAL PARK is famous for its wildlife, bubbling mud pots, and thundering geysers. But in 1988 it became famous for something else: world-class forest fires. Drought and lightning storms brought the biggest fire season in recorded history. In July, the lightning started fires that grew out of control and kept burning for four months. On the worst day during those months, winds drove fires across more than 150,000 acres of the park. By the end of the summer, 25,000 firefighters had worked to put out the fires, with as many as 9,000 on the scene at one time, but they could not control the wildfires. Only autumn snows brought things under control, and the last fires weren't out until the end of October.

The Yellowstone fires destroyed some buildings, but they also brought life. Fire is the way the Earth cleans out a forest. When fire clears the ground of dead brush, new trees and plants can grow where none lived before. Also, some trees have special qualities that help defend them in case of a wildfire. Douglas firs have thick bark to protect them from fire, and the cones of lodgepole pines are actually designed to open in the heat of fire, spreading new seeds. Aspen trees may burn to the ground, but their roots survive and they sprout saplings in no time.

Connection

By God's design, when a forest is cleared, it leaves land that is ripe for new forest life. Sometimes our lives seem like a raging fire, with angry hot spots between friends and family members. But Ephesians 4:26 says, "Don't sin by letting anger control you." If we treat each other lovingly in the midst of the fiery times, God can clear things out to bring new life to our relationships.

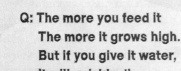 What Can I Do?

Respect *the power of fire.* Be careful. When you are out in the wilderness, put out campfires completely. Ask your parents to park the car away from dry forest areas where fuel leaks might accidentally start a fire. Avoid using matches inside your tent. In some areas, park rangers clear brush from the ground to let more natural forest growth happen, and they often ask for volunteers. You can help!

Riddle

Q: The more you feed it
   The more it grows high.
   But if you give it water,
   It will quickly die.
   What is it?

A: Fire.

The Strongest Storms on Earth

Do you know how God controls the storm and causes the
lightning to flash from his clouds? Do you understand how he
moves the clouds with wonderful perfection and skill?
JOB 37:15-16

HURRICANES ARE the strongest storms on Earth. They form
as swirls of warm and cool air meet over the ocean. Heat from
warm seawater strengthens them into violent whirlpools hundreds
of miles across.

On the morning of August 23, 2005, astronauts aboard the International Space Station looked down on a pretty swirl of clouds near
the Bahamas. Within days, the little swirl had blossomed into one
of the most deadly storms in American history: Hurricane Katrina.
It moved across the Bahamas, Cuba, and Florida, gaining strength
as it went. On August 29, the storm slammed into the Gulf Coast
states. Its 150 mph winds destroyed buildings and flooded many
towns and cities, including New Orleans. By the time the hurricane
died out, 2,500 people were dead or missing, and 80 percent of
New Orleans was beneath floodwaters.

The Breton National Wildlife Refuge is made up of two small
islands off the coast of Louisiana. It is the nesting ground for many
seabirds, including the endangered brown pelican. The wildlife
refuge took a direct hit from Hurricane Katrina. Wildlife biologists
worked frantically to rescue as many newly hatched pelicans as
they could, but many didn't make it. Their island home was all but
destroyed. Over the next years, people worked hard to rebuild and
revegetate this area. As of July 2009, there were 2,000 brown pelican
nests counted on the islands. That is great news! If you want to find
out more about the brown pelicans at the Breton Refuge, go to
http://www.fws.gov/breton/pelican_web/pelican_links.html.

Connection

Hurricanes and other natural forces show us the mighty power of God. Proverbs reminds us of this when it says, "Who has gathered up the wind in the hollow of his hands?" (Proverbs 30:4, NIV). God is powerful, but he is also merciful and gentle. Just like the workers at Breton National Wildlife Refuge are rebuilding and replanting the islands, God restores us after we go through hard times in our lives.

What Can I Do?

Reflect on God's power. For more about storms and the power of God, look in the book of Job, especially chapters 36–41.

Fun Fact

Each year, meteorologists name every hurricane in alphabetical order, skipping names beginning with *q, u, x, y,* and *z.* In 2005, for the first time, there were 27 hurricanes to name. Meteorologists used up the entire alphabet, then began naming storms after Greek letters!

Joke

Q: **What did one hurricane say to the other hurricane?**

A: **"I've got my eye on you."**

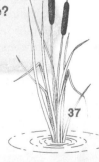

DAY 19 A Rocky Slip 'n' Slide

A great earthquake struck—the worst since people were placed on the earth. The great city of Babylon split into three sections, and the cities of many nations fell into heaps of rubble.
REVELATION 16:18-19

IT WAS THE SPRING OF 2008, and the people of China were preparing to host the Summer Olympic Games. On May 12, three months before the Olympics were to begin, the world fell apart. At least that's how it felt to hundreds of thousands of people in the Sichuan province of China when an earthquake rolled through the countryside. It toppled buildings, burst dams, and buried villages. This massive quake killed 69,000 people.

We like to think of the ground under our feet as solid and stable, but there's a whole lot of moving and shaking going on down there. Rivers of water gurgle underground, while rivers of magma (melted rock) flow beneath us. Massive rocks slip and slide, and when they do, they cause earthquakes. Earthquakes are a side effect of the tectonics that keep our world moving. (For more on tectonics, see day #10.)

The Chinese government planned to spend $146 billion to repair schools, collapsed highways and bridges, public buildings, and homes in Sichuan. Many nations sent relief workers, money, food, and construction materials into earthquake areas to help out. China was still able to host athletes from around the world for the XXIX Olympic Games.

 Connection

In the book of Revelation, God tells us that he sometimes uses earthquakes to destroy evil. Chapter 16 describes a quake near the end of the world that is part of his judgment against sin. God can also use earthquakes to help people, just as he did to free Paul and Silas from prison when they were singing praise songs (see Acts 16:22-26).

 **What Can I Do?**

Reflect on new ideas. Remember these tips if you are ever in an earthquake: If you are inside, take cover under a heavy piece of furniture, like a strong desk. You can also stand against a wall away from glass windows or skylights that might break. Stay inside until the ground stops shaking! If you are outside, move out into the open, away from buildings, streetlights, and overhead power lines.

 Factoid

The deadliest earthquake ever recorded shook the Earth in Shansi, China, on January 23, 1556. Over 830,000 people died in the earthquake and the tidal waves that came afterward.

Surf's Up!

I, the LORD, define the ocean's sandy shoreline
as an everlasting boundary that the waters cannot cross.
The waves may toss and roar, but they can
never pass the boundaries I set.
JEREMIAH 5:22

WHEN THERE IS a perfect wave, surfers call to their buddies, "Surf's up!" But sometimes the surf is just a little too "up." Undersea earthquakes or volcanoes can trigger monster waves called tidal waves or tsunamis. These waves are nasty: tsunamis can travel up to 500 mph, and they can cause severe damage to anything in their path.

The day after Christmas in 2004, there was a powerful earthquake on the ocean floor off the coast of Sumatra. This earthquake resulted in a tsunami that slammed into the beach of Sri Lanka, an island just south of India. The towering wave killed 35,000 people and left 443,000 with damaged or completely destroyed homes. The tsunami waves rolled across 11 countries in the region, leaving over 200,000 dead altogether.

Many nations rushed to the aid of Sri Lanka. The World Bank sent millions of dollars to rebuild homes, schools, and roads. Volunteers from all over the world brought a new flood—a flood of compassion—to the island nation.

 Connection

Jesus had compassion on the hungry; he fed them (see Matthew 14:13-21). He had compassion on the sick; he healed them (see Matthew 8:1-4). Jesus had compassion on the lost; he helped them find their way back, like a loving shepherd (see Luke 15:1-7). When disaster strikes, Jesus has compassion.

 What Can I Do?

React *with compassion.* We may not be able to go to another part of the world when we hear about a tsunami or hurricane, but there are still things we can do. We can help people across the globe who are suffering by giving money to organizations like Samaritan's Purse and World Vision, which are directly involved in disaster relief.

✹ Amazing Fact

A British girl named Amber Mason and her family were visiting a resort in Phuket in Thailand, in the area where the tsunami hit. Amber was riding an elephant named Ningnong when they heard a huge wave roaring in from the ocean. Ningnong ran uphill as far as he could and then braced himself as the water swirled around his legs. Ningnong saved Amber from the rushing water.

Explosive Disasters

We tell others about Christ, warning everyone
and teaching everyone with all the wisdom God has given us.
COLOSSIANS 1:28

THE PEOPLE IN the city of Goma live in the shadow of a dangerous volcano. Goma is in the heart of the Democratic Republic of Congo in Africa, next to a volcano called Nyiragongo. Volcanoes make rich farmland, so Goma is surrounded by farms and crops of beans and maize (corn).

Nyiragongo has seven volcanic "brothers" next to it, all part of the Virunga Mountains. In the crater atop Nyiragongo lies a lake of lava. In late 2001 and early 2002, the mountain began to smoke and many earthquakes shook the area, giving people a warning that something was up inside the volcano. On January 17, 2002, molten rock poured from the volcano toward the city below. More than 400,000 people had to be evacuated as lava reached the outskirts of Goma. Lava destroyed 4,500 buildings and even covered one end of the main runway at Goma's airport! But thanks to scientists who saw the warning signs, the people of Goma were able to flee in time.

Joke

Q: What did one volcano say to the other volcano?

A: "I lava you."

 Connection

People who live near Nyiragongo have fine farms with lush vegetation. But they must always be watchful of the dangers that can come from the mountain next door. There are things in our lives that we must be watchful about too. In 1 Peter 5:8, we are warned that we need to be "self-controlled and alert" (NIV), and 1 Corinthians 16:13 says to "be on your guard" (NIV). Why? So that we can be strong in our faith, always enjoying the good things God gives us and staying away from those things that can lead us away from him.

What Can I Do?

Relay *your thoughts to God.* Pray for the people of Goma and others who live in danger zones—for their protection and healing.

Explosive Fact

Mount Nyiragongo has erupted at least 34 times since 1882.

Powerful Fact

Energy companies in California have built power plants that run on volcanic steam. This geothermal energy is renewable and nonpolluting.

The LORD is slow to anger and great in power. . . .
His way is in the whirlwind and the storm,
and clouds are the dust of his feet.
NAHUM 1:3, NIV

TORNADOES "STAR" in many movies. Scientists watch in horror as a twister carries cows and giant trucks through the air. A funnel-shaped storm transports Dorothy and Toto from Kansas to Oz. Can tornadoes really do these things? These movie depictions aren't that much of an exaggeration. The fact is, tornadoes are so powerful that they have been known to force pieces of straw into solid wood and pick up train cars as if they were toys.

Tornadoes begin when cool air high up in the atmosphere begins to sink toward the ground. If the ground is warm enough, hot air rises. When cool meets warm, the atmosphere mixes in a whirlpool of air. Once it gets going, a tornado can drive winds up to 300 mph.

Tornadoes move through the air like serpents, bobbing and twisting as they touch the ground. That's why they're often called twisters. Wherever they hit land, they can destroy buildings, cars, and farmland. If you hear that tornadoes have been spotted in your area, head for the basement and listen to the TV or radio to know when it's safe to come out.

 Connection

Just because we are Christians doesn't mean that disasters skip us. Sometimes our lives feel like a confusing tornado spinning out of control—not because of the weather but because of what's going on inside of us. Proverbs 10:25 tells us, "When the storms of life come, the wicked are whirled away, but the godly have a lasting foundation." While disaster can happen to anyone, people who trust in Jesus have a strong foundation to hold on to in the middle of life's storms. Jesus is strong and unchanging.

 **What Can I Do?**

Rethink *your pantry.* If you live in a region where tornadoes occur, store a few days' worth of food in your basement or storm shelter. Then if local stores or roads get damaged, you will have food to eat and to share with others. Canned goods, bottled water, juice, and dry goods like crackers and dried fruit will be good for months.

 Scary Factoid

The worst tornado in history rumbled across Missouri, Illinois, and Indiana in 1925. It left a deadly track at least 219 miles long. This monster storm was nearly a mile wide! By the time it was over, 695 people were dead and 15,000 homes destroyed.

45

DAY 23
Is the Earth Getting Warmer?

All the earth is the LORD's, and he has set the world in order.
1 SAMUEL 2:8

GLOBAL WARMING IS a hot topic these days. Most scientists believe the Earth is in a warming trend, but not all can agree on the cause. It's true that if the world's average temperature increased too much, the ice at Earth's poles would melt, raising ocean levels and drenching beach cities around the world. Some island communities in the tropics have had to be evacuated in recent years due to rising water levels, and large parts of Antarctica's ice shelf have broken off.

One thing that contributes to higher temperatures is something called greenhouse gas. Greenhouse gases act just like a greenhouse: they let sunlight in but change it to heat so that it stays in and warms the air. The same effect happens in a car, as sunlight passes through glass windows, changes into heat, and can't get out again, so it melts your favorite candy bar on the front seat. Greenhouse gases include carbon dioxide, carbon monoxide, and other gases that come out of our factories and cars. Greenhouse gases come from natural sources, too. People debate whether global warming is caused by humans or by natural trends, but it certainly can be aggravated by the way we treat the Earth, so it is wise for us to not pump greenhouse gases into the air if we can help it.

Here are some things to think about: The last two decades of the 20th century were the hottest in 400 years. Although not every area of the world is warmer, the average global temperature has increased. Polar bears hunt on the ice, but arctic ice is disappearing fast. The bears are having such a hard time hunting that they have now been put on the "threatened species" list. Montana's Glacier

National Park had 150 glaciers in 1910. Today, it has only 27. The rest have melted away! Coral reefs are sensitive to small rises in water temperature. In the last five years, huge sections of these underwater gardens have died due to warmer temperatures.

♻ Connection

As 1 Samuel 2:8 says, everything on this planet belongs to God, and when it comes down to it, he's ultimately the one in control of what happens here. But he has also called us to look after his "garden" since the days of Eden. That means we have a responsibility to protect our air from greenhouse gases, preserve air-cleaning forests, and keep our waterways and wilderness areas free from pollution. We need to be part of the solution, not part of the problem.

What Can I Do?

Rethink *how you can make a difference.* God has designed our environment so that plants absorb greenhouse gases. Ask your parents if you can plant a tree in the yard, or volunteer to help with community and park projects that plant trees in public areas.

Joke

Q: What do you call it when worms take over the world?

A: Global worming.

Spotting the Trends

You know the saying, "Red sky at night means fair weather tomorrow; red sky in the morning means foul weather all day." You know how to interpret the weather signs in the sky.
MATTHEW 16:2-3

THE WEATHER CHANGES from season to season, but each year the trends are similar. The temperature and weather of a certain location over a long period is called climate. For example, the band of Earth along the equator stays warm all year round because it gets the most sunlight throughout the entire year. This is called a tropical climate. Desert climates have low rainfall. Polar climates have cold temperatures. The long-term patterns of these places make each one unique.

Climate change means that the world's climate trends are gradually shifting. The Earth has experienced climate change before: the northern part of the United States was buried under thousands of feet of ice just a few thousand years ago. Now, however, some areas of the world are warming up. Glaciers are shrinking in about 80 percent of the world's cold areas. Sea life is changing in places where ocean water is warmer than it used to be. Mosquitoes are spreading to areas that used to be too cold for them. Many scientists believe these things add up to one conclusion: the world's climate is warming up. Others feel that our records do not go back far enough to tell for sure and that the real changes we see may be small variations in climate rather than a new "hot" trend. It is important to watch and study the Earth's weather patterns and climate to understand these things. As caretakers of God's world, we must pay attention to the environment so we can treat it responsibly.

 ## Connection

When Jesus spoke about the sky in Matthew 16, he was talking about more than the weather. He was telling his listeners to watch for the signs that God's Kingdom was near. He also talked about signs to watch for that would show he was coming back. When Jesus does return, what kind of world will he see? Will we be proud of how we took care of God's creation?

 ## What Can I Do?

Reflect *on new ideas.* Along with your parents, pay attention to the news so you can keep up with what's happening with the environment. This is one way you can be a responsible helper to God in caring for his "garden," the Earth.

Factoid

The major climates of the world are: tropical rainforest, savanna, desert, steppe, chaparral, grasslands, deciduous forest, taiga, tundra, and alpine. For details on what these different climates are like, a great Web site is http://www.blueplanetbiomes.org/climate.htm.

Joke

Q: How do you get to the top of a tree?

A: You climate.

The Little Ice Age

God's breath sends the ice,
freezing wide expanses of water.
JOB 37:10

DID YOU KNOW there was a mini ice age that lasted at least 250 years, ending in the 1850s? Europe and North America had terribly cold winters. Glaciers moved down through the Swiss Alps, gradually crushing villages. In China, it became too cold to grow citrus fruit. Crops all over the world failed, and many people starved.

What caused the Little Ice Age? No one is sure. One guess is that it was a combination of two things: First, there was decreased solar activity—the sun was just not putting out as many warming rays. Second, many volcanoes erupted during this time. One example was the volcano Tambora in Indonesia, which erupted in 1815. The ash from this volcano spread to cover most of the world, blocking out the sun for over a year. That's why 1816, the year after Tambora erupted, was called "the year without a summer." It was so cold that it snowed in June and July in New England and parts of Europe.

Connection

There are some things that we have a degree of control over and plenty of others that we don't. The weather changes, climates change, and circumstances change. Only God stays the same. As it says in Hebrews 13:8, "Jesus Christ is the same yesterday, today, and forever."

What Can I Do?

Record *the temperature.* In a small notebook, keep track of the high and low temperatures each day for one week. Thank God that even when other things in your life change, he stays the same.

 **Fun Fact**

In 1780, during the Little Ice Age, New York Harbor froze solid, and instead of taking the ferry, people walked across the ice from Manhattan to Staten Island.

Joke

Q: Why did the woman go outside with her purse open?

A: Because she expected some change in the air.

Fun Quote

"Everybody is talking about the weather but nobody does anything about it."
— MARK TWAIN

DAY 26 Bug Spray Gone Bad

Not a single sparrow can fall to the ground
without your Father knowing it.
MATTHEW 10:29

PEOPLE ARE LEARNING how a single man-made change can
affect the environment. Here is one "oops" example. About
100 years ago, scientists invented a pesticide called DDT. It helped
kill off mosquitoes that spread malaria, a flu-like disease that is
often fatal. Then farmers around the world started using DDT to
kill the insects that were eating up their crops. So there was less
malaria and more food for everyone. That's good, right? Yes, but
as the years went by, scientists noticed that bird populations were
dying off. They soon figured out why. Birds who ate insects that
had been sprayed with DDT laid eggs with weak shells. The shells
often broke before the eggs could hatch. And since DDT killed good
insects as well as harmful ones, the birds that did hatch couldn't
find enough insects to eat. Soon doctors also realized that the DDT
was poisoning the people who used it on their crops. What a mess!

DDT was banned in many countries about 30 years ago, and it
has been replaced with safer pesticides. Now the bird populations
are coming back.

 Connection

When it comes to doing the right thing, people usually
mean well. But sometimes an action done with the best
of intentions can cause disaster. As it says in Psalm
73:22-24, "I was so foolish and ignorant—I must have
seemed like a senseless animal to you. Yet I still belong
to you; you hold my right hand. You guide me with your
counsel." Can you think of a time when you did something
that you thought would be good and helpful, and it turned into
a big mess? We can also create a mess of our lives by doing wrong
things—which the Bible calls sin. But God's goodness is bigger than
any chaos we can make of our lives. There is no mess too big for God
to clean up.

 What Can I Do?

Rethink *what you spray.* Some insecticides can be harmful to the
creatures that eat insects. To get rid of aphids (little plant-eating
insects), you can plant marigolds, which attract aphid-eating lady-
bugs, or you can wash the aphids off of plants with your water hose.
Commercial weed killers can also cause problems for birds and
beneficial insects. Here is a recipe for natural, cheap weed killer.
Put the following in a big spray bottle:

> 1 quart vinegar
> ¼ cup salt
> 1 teaspoon liquid dish soap

Shake the bottle until the salt dissolves. Spray on weeds in rock
beds, along sidewalks, and beside the driveway. Don't spray on
grass!

A Spill That Took 20 Years to Clean Up

Do not pollute the land where you are.
NUMBERS 35:33, NIV

OIL IS A fossil fuel that comes from deep inside the ground. (Scientists call these substances fossil fuels because they are made of ancient plants and animals.) People refine or purify oil to make gasoline, plastic, and even medicine. Every day, supertankers steam across the world's oceans, carrying oil to where it's needed. Most tankers arrive safely in port. But from 1964 to 2004, there were five major oil spills around the world. In those cases, super-tankers developed leaks or broke apart, flooding the sea with oil. One of these disasters happened off the coast of Alaska in 1989.

Late one night, the *Exxon Valdez* supertanker turned to avoid an iceberg and hit some rocks. The hull ripped open, and 11 million gallons of oil poured into the water. The thick, sludgy oil washed up on Alaska's beaches and coastline, killing at least 250 bald eagles, 22 killer whales, 300 seals, 2,800 sea otters, and 250,000 seabirds.

Some animals were poisoned by the oil. Others died of cold—the oil coated their fur and feathers so they had no way to trap warm air next to their skin to keep warm. Some animals starved to death because the oil traveled down the food chain, killing the coastal clams, snails, and worms that these animals ate.

Workers saved as many shoreline animals as they could. They took them to shelters, where they used dishwashing liquid to clean off the oil. Then the animals were kept in cages until they were healthy enough to be released.

Scientists are learning how to prevent oil spills. New rules say that all supertankers need double hulls so the oil won't go directly into the ocean if one of the hulls leaks. People are also discovering new ways to clean up when a spill does occur. Floating barriers called booms

(think of a gigantic chain of buoys) can corral the oil and keep it from

spreading. Then the oil can be sucked up with special hoses.
Or the oil can be set on fire to burn it up and get it out of the water.
Certain chemicals can be poured on the oil to turn it into tiny droplets
so it does much less damage. Straw or sawdust can also be spread on
the oil, soaking it up off the surface of the water like giant sponges.

Connection

It took almost 20 years for nature to undo the damage done by the
Exxon Valdez oil spill. Sin can cause serious damage too. If we don't
deal with our sin, it can spread and hurt us and others for a long
time. The verse at the beginning of this devotion is talking about the
land becoming polluted by people's violence to each other. But our
hearts can also become polluted when we do things that go against
what God wants us to do.

What Can I Do?

Respect *God's world.* One of the most damaging substances to the
environment is oil, whether it's caused by a sinking ship or a family
car. See if you can help by finding out where your family can safely
get rid of oil. Auto shops often recycle oil to keep it from harming
the environment.

Crazy Fact

Scientists are designing a bacterium that eats up oil and toxic chemicals. The snazzy scientific word for this technique is *bioremediation.*

DAY
28 **The Disappearing Lake**

Anyone who is thirsty may come to me!
Anyone who believes in me may come and drink!
For the Scriptures declare,
"Rivers of living water will flow from his heart."
JOHN 7:37-38

IF YOU'VE EVER been on a long car trip, you know how great it
is to find a rest stop. For tired migrating birds in the western
United States, California's Mono Lake provides just the place to
stop and rest awhile. This salt lake is fed by six streams and serves
as a bird restaurant and nesting ground. It's a delicate place, in just
the right balance. Even small changes can damage it. In fact, a few
decades ago, the lake began to die.

Los Angeles County needed more water for its growing cities, so
it began to take water from some of the streams that fed the lake.
Soon Mono Lake began to dry up. As it did, its water became salt-
ier, and the brine shrimp and other aquatic life that fed the birds
began to die off. Something else happened too. Birds had always
used the islands in the middle of the lake as safe nesting grounds.
But as Mono's water level lowered, a land bridge opened up from
the shore to one of the islands. Now predators could get to the
island, so the birds had to give up their safe haven.

But Mono Lake became a success story. Environmentalists and
the park service convinced Los Angeles that Mono Lake was an
important natural place that needed protection. Today Los Angeles
gets its water from other sources. The lake is slowly filling again,
giving wildlife an important roadside stop.

 Connection

As Jesus said in today's verse, God's love and energy are like "living water" to you. If your living water gets too low, and your energy cup empties out, it opens up a dangerous pathway for life to distract you from God's plans. Just like physical water keeps us alive and refreshes our bodies, Jesus, the living water, gives life and refreshment to our spirits. And unlike Mono Lake, his living water will never dry up.

 What Can I Do?

Reduce *your water usage.* It's all about water. Mono Lake began to die because people were taking water from its streams. We can help the environment by cutting back on the water we use. Here is one cool way: take a four-minute shower. This can save eight gallons of fresh water every time you shower! (See day #74 for more details.)

 **Fun Fact**

Bizarre-looking towers of salt, called tufas, ring the shores of Mono Lake. They look so strange that many Westerns and sci-fi movies have been filmed there. The Dead Sea of the Bible lands has similar columns.

Air Pollution Solutions

Let us cleanse ourselves from everything
that can defile our body or spirit.
2 CORINTHIANS 7:1

S MOG IS A MIX of smoke and fog. In 1952, London experienced the famous "Killer Smog." This is what happened. Usually smoke from the coal-burning stoves the Londoners used drifted up into the air and blew away. But one day a heavy fog moved into the city. The smoke mixed with the fog and did not blow away. A layer of warm air above the fog held the smog in place for four awful days. The heavy, smelly yellow smog turned day into night. Men with lanterns walked in front of cars and buses to guide them through the gloom. Thousands of Londoners died from breathing the smog. A few years later, in 1956, Great Britain passed the Clean Air Act, which limited the burning of coal.

Smoke from household fires is still a terrible pollution problem in developing countries. About half the people in the world make indoor fires from wood and animal dung to prepare meals. These cook fires release dangerous levels of soot, carbon dioxide, carbon monoxide, and other toxic fumes into the air of the hut or house. In fact, the World Health Organization rates indoor air pollution as one of the top 10 causes of death worldwide.

Envirofit International, a nonprofit company based in Fort Collins, Colorado, has come up with a creative solution to this problem. They have designed affordable, clean-burning cookstoves to sell to people in developing countries. The stoves' efficient airflow concentrates the heat so that food cooks faster, and it puts out

58 80 percent less smoke than regular cooking fires.

Connection

Have you ever heard the phrase *too much of a good thing*? Carbon dioxide is what plants breathe. But if there's too much of it in the ocean, the water becomes acidic and ocean plants die. Too much carbon dioxide also fosters acid rain, which damages rivers and crops. Carbon dioxide can be a case of too much of a good thing in our outside environment. We can have the same thing happen in our everyday lives. Do you like to watch movies? Great! But watching them all day turns you into a couch potato. Do you like candy? A little is fine, but a lot gives you holes in your teeth! Proverbs 25:16 says, "Do you like honey? Don't eat too much, or it will make you sick!"

What Can I Do?

Rethink *what you put into the air.* There are many simple, easy ways to make our air cleaner. Here is one idea. Does your family use a charcoal grill to barbecue? Ask your parents if you can have a garage sale to make money to buy a gas grill instead. Using a gas grill will help keep a lot of smoke out of the air.

 Fun Fact

In 1272, King Edward I of England made the first air pollution law. He ruled that Londoners could not burn "sea-coal"—coal that came from other countries and produced a tremendous amount of smoke.

59

The trees of the LORD are well cared for—
the cedars of Lebanon that he planted.
PSALM 104:16

GOD MADE FORESTS to be the "lungs" of the Earth. Forests produce oxygen for us to breathe, and they clean the carbon dioxide out of the air. They also play an important role in the weather. Trees take up water through their roots and release it into the air through their leaves. The moisture they release from their leaves gathers into clouds in the sky, which release the moisture again in the form of rain. When forests are cut down, our Earth is damaged in many ways. Areas that were once lush and green become dry and desertlike. There is less oxygen in the air because there are fewer trees. Animals die off with the loss of their habitat. Eventually there aren't enough creatures in that area to decay and turn into new soil when they die. When it rains or floods, mud slides carry the old soil away since there are no tree roots to hold it in place.

Forests also provide homes for thousands of species of animals. Experts guess that over 80 percent of the world's animal species are still undiscovered and that many of these creatures live in remote tropical forests. But as the Earth's population grows, more and more forests in developing countries are being cut down. New trees don't grow fast enough to replace the trees that are being cut down.

What can be done to protect these forests? Richer countries can provide financial support for developing countries so they won't have to cut down their forests. Instead of cutting down trees, countries like Costa Rica make money through ecotourism—providing tours of their tropical rain forests. Some nonprofit agencies buy natural forests to protect them from being destroyed.

Connection

Jesus commanded us: "Love your neighbor as yourself" (Matthew 22:39). If we here in the United States can help developing countries find new ways to make a living without having to cut down their forests, we are being good neighbors to them. It's a way to show love to them, just as we'd want them to do for us.

What Can I Do?

Research *ways you can help.* Organizations such as the Nature Conservancy are working to protect our world's wild places. Take a look at their Web site: http://www.nature.org/initiatives/forests. If you like what they are doing, you can send some of your allowance money or birthday money to help conserve forests around the world. There is also a page on the Web site that tells you where you can volunteer to help care for wild areas near your community.

Fun Fact

There are about 100,000 different species of trees. Trees make up about 25 percent of all living plants.

Joke

Q: What kind of tree can fit in your hand?

A: A palm tree.

Do You Have a Dinosaur in Your Tank?

DAY 31

By wisdom the LORD founded the earth;
by understanding he created the heavens.
PROVERBS 3:19

DO YOU KNOW the first way people made energy, before there were things like cars and electricity and air-conditioning? People long ago burned wood for heat and light. Since then people have discovered other things that can be burned to make energy: oil, coal, and natural gas. We use natural gas to cook with and to heat our homes. We use oil to power cars, ships, and airplanes.

People need to dig deep into the Earth to get oil, coal, and natural gas. These three heat sources are all fossil fuels—rich substances made from the fossilized remains of plants and animals. But these fossil fuels are nonrenewable, which means that once they get used up, they will be gone for good.

Think about this: some of the gas in your car could be leftovers from a T. rex!

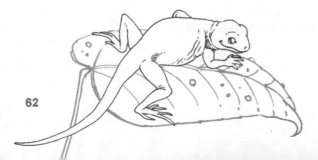

62

Connection

God gave us humans intelligent brains to think with. All of us can use our God-given thinking abilities to find new and creative sources of energy as we use up old sources that can't be replaced. Proverbs 2:6 tells us, "The LORD grants wisdom! From his mouth come knowledge and understanding."

 What Can I Do?

Rethink your transportation. You may not be able to drive yet, but you can save gas! Instead of having your parents drive you places, try walking or riding your bike. You can ask your parents to carpool when you and your friends are headed to the same activity. You and your family can also have fun exploring public transportation (subways and buses) if you live in a city. Some cities even have light-rail trains that are run by electricity. Finding new ways to travel isn't just good for the world God made—it's also fun!

News Flash

The average American uses 500 gallons of gas each year.

Tongue Twister

Say this five times fast: "Fossil-fuel free."

Disneyland's Green Train

Smoke streams from its nostrils like steam
from a pot heated over burning rushes.
JOB 41:20

WHEN DISNEYLAND OPENED IN 1955, one of its first rides was the steam train, which still takes people all around the park. The train is powered by steam, but until recently, that steam came from water heated by diesel fuel. Now, however, the Disneyland Railroad has gone green . . . with the help of a little fast food.

After making their french fries, cooks in Disneyland kitchens ship their used canola oil to a nearby processing plant. At the plant, the cooking oil is turned into biofuel, which "burns clean" (meaning it doesn't put much pollution into the air). The Disneyland Railroad is still a steam engine, but now its water is heated by clean biofuel. Disneyland estimates that the process saves 200,000 gallons of diesel fuel every year. And soon, the same fuel will power even more rides in this magical park.

♻ Connection

When water boils and turns to steam, it can move heavy things with its unseen power. Like steam, the Spirit of God can't be seen, but he gives us power to do the right things and live a joyful life. Romans 8:2 says, "Because you belong to him, the power of the life-giving Spirit has freed you."

What Can I Do?

Rejoice in God's power. Thank God that he is stronger than any other kind of power there is. The next time you're facing a tough situation, ask him for his help and his power.

☀ Fun Fact

Steam power has been used for over 2,000 years, but it really got going 300 years ago, when it was first used to run tractors, trains, and boats.

Joke

Q: How can you tell when a train is eating?

A: You can hear it chooing.

New Ideas for New Energy

> The ground is cursed because of you. All your life you
> will struggle to scratch a living from it. It will grow thorns and
> thistles for you, though you will eat of its grains. By the sweat
> of your brow will you have food to eat.
> GENESIS 3:17-19

ADAM AND EVE didn't need to hunt for sources of heat and light and power when they were living in the Garden of Eden—God provided them with everything they needed. But ever since they got booted out of Eden, we humans have been scurrying around our planet in a constant search for energy: energy to stay warm, cook our food, and get us from point A to point B.

For hundreds of years people have burned wood and coal to keep warm and to make energy for running machines like coal-engine trains and steamships. Over the last 150 years, people have been burning oil and natural gas (fossil fuels) to stay warm and to power planes, trains, and cars.

Now scientists and engineers are working on other options besides fossil fuels. They're trying to come up with new ways to create energy *and* clean up the environment at the same time. One idea that's being tried out is biofuel, a type of fuel made from crops. Biofuel burns clean—it puts out very little pollution. The challenge about biofuel is that it's expensive to make, so it doesn't have as much "bang for your buck" as regular gas. A gallon of ethanol (a fuel made from corn or sugarcane) has only about two-thirds as much energy in it as a gallon of gasoline. A gallon of biodiesel (often made from soybeans) has three-fourths as much energy as a gallon of gas. Right now, 100 percent biofuel can only be used in special "flex-fuel" cars. But as engineers continue to make improvements and come up with new ideas, who knows what you may be filling your tank with in 10 years!

 Connection

Scientists are looking for new sources of energy to power our machines. As Christians, we know where *our* source of energy comes from: God (see 2 Corinthians 12:9). We were created with "spiritual tanks" that need to be filled every day. We fill our tanks by talking to God, worshiping him, and reading his Word. Nothing else will fill up our tanks and give us the God-created "fuel" we need—not movies, computer games, friends, food, or any stuff we could buy. Only God is the real deal; only he can give us the energy we need to be who we were created to be.

 What Can I Do?

Relay your thoughts to God. "As I read this book, teach me more about your world and how I can help take care of it. Please give me creative ideas about how to protect all the good things you've given us."

 Fun Fact

What living things have one cell, are green, grow in water, and can be turned into biofuel? Algae! Scientists think this may be the next big thing in "green" fuel. Algae grow much faster than land plants, and they can grow in ponds, seawater, or wastewater. Algae-based biofuel is currently being tested and has already provided fuel for a Boeing 737 test flight.

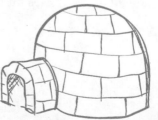

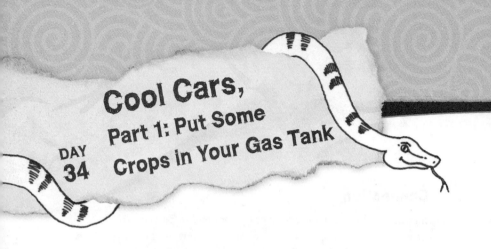

Cool Cars,
Part 1: Put Some Crops in Your Gas Tank

DAY 34

I am about to do something new.
See, I have already begun! Do you not see it?
I will make a pathway through the wilderness.
I will create rivers in the dry wasteland.
ISAIAH 43:19

WHEN PEOPLE ARE getting ready to leave, they might use the old joke, "Let's make like a tree and leaf." With biofuel, cars can actually "make like trees" because of what's in their tanks. How? The answer is ethanol, the fuel mentioned on day #33. This fuel is made from corn or other plants. When ethanol is mixed with normal gasoline, it makes the gas burn cleaner. Most gasoline at the gas pump these days is about 10 percent ethanol. Special flex-fuel cars can use a mix of 15 percent gasoline and 85 percent ethanol, and these E85 cars put out less pollution than regular cars.

Ethanol comes from crops grown in the United States, which means we can buy less oil from other countries. And because it is grown from plants, it is a renewable energy source, unlike gas and oil. Each year, more and more E85 cars hit the roads.

♻️ Connection

Using crops seems like a surprising way to fuel our cars, but it's a great solution. In the same way, God often uses surprising new things to work out his purposes. Today's verse talks about God's plans to do "something new." Who would have guessed that the Savior of the world would be born in a stable? Do you think God might be doing something surprising in your life too?

🗑️ What Can I Do?

Relay *your thoughts to God.* "Lord, thank you for the creative ways people are reducing pollution in your creation. Help me to be creative about that too—both now and when I grow up!"

☀️ Factoid

In 2004, ethanol reduced car pollution by 7 million tons. That's the same as removing a million cars from the road!

Jokes

Q: What happens to old mufflers?
A: They get exhausted.

Q: When is a car not a car?
A: When it turns into a driveway.

Cool Cars, Part 2: Hybrids

Though one may be overpowered, two can defend themselves.
ECCLESIASTES 4:12, NIV

SOMETIMES PUTTING two things together creates something stronger than each of the two were on their own. What happens when you put a gas-powered engine with an electric one? You get . . . the Insight. The Prius. The Volt. These are all hybrid cars. And what does that mean, exactly?

A regular car burns gasoline to make power. A spark ignites a small amount of gasoline inside a metal cylinder. The small explosion moves a piston, which rotates the wheels of the car. Most cars have four or six of these cylinders, and the explosions inside them go off about a hundred times a minute. A gallon of gas weighs about six pounds. A regular car turns that gas into 20 pounds of greenhouse gases (carbon dioxide and carbon monoxide).

A hybrid car also uses gas, but part of its power comes from clean electricity. Hybrid cars have two motors instead of one: a gas-burning motor and an electric motor. The electric motor works at slow speeds and runs on a battery. When the car's speed gets up to about 40 mph, the regular motor kicks in for extra power. While the gas motor is on, it also charges the battery for the electric motor. Because of this combination, hybrid cars use far less gas and pollute the air less.

A gas-powered Honda Civic—an efficient and inexpensive car—goes about 35 miles on a gallon of gas, while a hybrid Honda Insight goes nearly 50 miles. Hybrid cars are expensive, but as more of them are made, they are gradually becoming cheaper. Hybrids promise to make our air a lot cleaner and our world a lot greener.

♻ Connection

A car can be made better by combining two things into one.
In the same way, Christ followers are stronger together than apart.
As Ecclesiastes 4:12 says, friends can help each other in hard times.

 ## What Can I Do?

Reduce your gas. Make a list of people who live near you. Then
make another list of places you drive to. Are there people on your
list who drive to the same places you do? Maybe you can carpool!

 ## News Flash

Today there are more than a million hybrid cars in the United
States . . . out of a total of 251 million U.S. cars.

Brain Quiz

1. **What is under the hood of a hybrid car?**
   a) A steam engine
   b) A combination gasoline engine and electric motor
   c) A flux capacitor that runs on banana peels
      and cardboard

2. **A typical SUV gets around 15 miles per gallon.**
   How many mpg can a hybrid get?
   a) 10 mpg
   b) 20 mpg
   c) 30 mpg

Answers: 1=b; 2=c

71

Cool Cars, Part 3: Electric Cars

With great power the apostles continued
to testify to the resurrection of the Lord Jesus,
and much grace was upon them.
ACTS 4:33, NIV

ELON MUSK is a creative man. He invented PayPal and started a rocket company called SpaceX. These days, he's planning cars powered by electricity. Unlike hybrids, his cars won't need any gas at all. Just plug in and play.

The first electric car Musk invented for the public is a sports car called the Tesla Roadster. This hot little car can go fast and far, driving 244 miles before it needs to be recharged. The cost of this trip is only a few dollars! The Tesla Roadster is expensive, but there are plans in the works for Tesla sedans—family cars that will carry more people for less money. Over 1,200 Roadsters have already been sold, and the family "Model S" cars will begin production in 2011.

There are other experimental cars that drive on electricity, but they don't go very fast and they can't go very far without needing to be plugged in for hours to be recharged. Instead of needing a charging site (like a gas station for electric cars), Tesla cars can be plugged in to the normal electrical current of a house with a special adapter.

Tesla Motors is also working with Daimler to make an electric Smart car. Electric cars may be the way of the future. Shocking, isn't it?

 Connection

The Tesla Roadster is a hot car. It can zip down the highway at lightning speed, but after about 240 miles it has to plug in to a power source before it can go any farther. In the book of Acts, the disciples operated this way too. They did wonderful things in the name of God, but they had to plug in to the Spirit's energy to do so—he was the source of their "great power." The same is true for us. When life is hard or we need to make an important decision, we need to plug in to the power of God's Holy Spirit. He loves us, and he has promised to give us his energy and wisdom if we ask.

 What Can I Do?

Relay your thoughts to God. God wants to be the source of strength and power in your life. You can do good things on your own for a while, but eventually you'll get tired of doing what's right. Keep in touch with God and let him be your power source.

Fun Fact

Experts estimate that in 2010 there will be 135,000 electric cars on U.S. roadways.

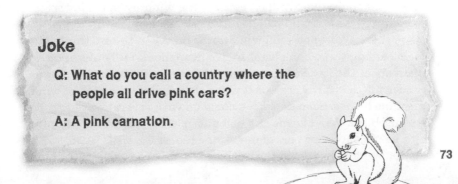

Joke

Q: What do you call a country where the people all drive pink cars?

A: A pink carnation.

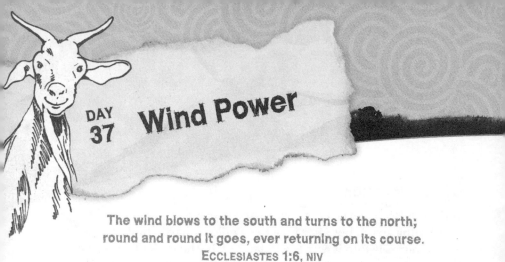

DAY 37 Wind Power

> The wind blows to the south and turns to the north;
> round and round it goes, ever returning on its course.
> ECCLESIASTES 1:6, NIV

DID YOU KNOW it's possible to make energy from moving air? It's a good idea, but it's not a new one. Ancient people captured the wind in sails to power their boats. The Persians built the oldest known windmills over a thousand years ago. They used them to pump water and grind grain. People in Holland have used windmills for hundreds of years to hold back the sea so they would have more farmland. In America's Western states, settlers in the 1800s depended on windmills for water for their homes and farms.

Heat from the sun makes the wind blow, so as long as we have the sun, we'll have wind. It's a renewable, unlimited source of clean energy that is starting to catch on around the world. Wind farms are made up of huge areas of land covered with wind machines. From far away, these areas look like a bunch of pinwheels stuck into the ground. Many of these machines are 20 stories high with two or three blades. A generator connected to the blades turns the wind energy into electricity. The electricity travels along underground cables and provides power to homes in the area.

What's not to like? Well . . . some of the windiest spots in the world are the most wild and beautiful. Some people want to preserve these areas, not build wind farms on them. Others think wind farms are ugly and don't want to live near them. Still others complain about the low humming noise the windmills make. Another concern is that birds are killed when they fly into the path of wind machine blades. Scientists have come up with several ways to solve this problem. Wind farms can be built in areas that are not hunting and nesting areas or part of migratory routes for birds. Also, special radar can shut down the engines if a flock of birds approaches.

Connection

Understanding the incredible power of the wind gives us a window into the awesome power of God. As the power of the wind can give us electricity, so the Holy Spirit blows through our lives, giving us the power to do what is right and turn away from what is wrong. Psalm 78:26 says, "He released the east wind in the heavens and guided the south wind by his mighty power."

 What Can I Do?

Rethink *your wattage.* Life without electricity has a whole different feel to it, and it's great to experience it. Ask your parents if you can take one 24-hour period without using any electricity at your house. Don't turn on electric lights, the TV, or computers. Cook meals outside on the grill, and light candles when it gets dark. Play board games instead of watching TV. Tell stories. Afterward, you can send us an e-mail and tell us what you thought about your "electricity-free" day. (See page 1 for our contact info.)

Fun Facts

- Wind power provides only half a percent of the total energy used in the United States.

- The states with the most wind production are Texas, California, Iowa, Minnesota, and Oklahoma.

Give thanks to him who made the heavenly lights . . . the sun
to rule the day, . . . and the moon and stars to rule the night.
PSALM 136:7-9

THANK GOD FOR the sun! This amazing star is the hottest
thing in our solar system. It puts out energy made from
nuclear fusion (hydrogen atoms crashing together and exploding
into helium). This energy shoots out from the sun as heat and light.
It travels at a dizzying speed. The sun is 93 million miles from
Earth, but its light reaches our planet in only eight minutes. Since
ancient times, people have tried to harness the sun's energy. The
ancient Pueblo people built their cliff dwellings facing south, allow-
ing the rocks to soak up the rays of the low winter sun. These early
versions of solar homes stayed warm in the winter. In the summer
they stayed cool, protected by the cliffs from the sun high overhead.

Fast-forward 2,000 years. Now people have learned new ways to
use solar power for homes. Flat, bluish solar panels are showing up
on more roofs every day. Here's how they work: water is circulated
through the panels, gets heated by the sun, and gives the household
hot water. People are also inventing tools to store the sun's energy.
Do you have a solar calculator? It is probably powered by small
photovoltaic cells. These doodads are made of silicon, which comes
from sand. They capture the sun's power and store it in batteries.

But there is still a lot left to learn about solar energy. Solar
power plants are expensive to build. They only work when the
sun is shining, so they can only be built in areas that get massive
amounts of sunshine year-round. They also take up a lot of room,
so they have to be built where there is open space. In spite of these
challenges, scientists are determined to figure out ways to capture
this power. There is so much potentially free energy beaming down
76 on us from the sun—we just have to figure out how to tap into it.

 Connection

Psalm 136 tells us that God made the sun to rule the day. He also gave us his Son, Jesus, to rule in our lives. God's Word gives us light so we can see the truth. His love gives us warmth to make us safe and secure. We can capture these things in our hearts every day.

What Can I Do?

Reflect *on the sun.* Go outside and feel the sun on your face. Being outdoors is a great reminder to thank God for the gift of our warm sun. We can soak it in, just like solar cells do.

Fun Sites

Check out these Web sites to learn more about solar energy:
  http://www.solarnow.org
  http://www.eia.doe.gov/kids/energyfacts/sources/renewable/
    solar.html
  http://www.solarenergy.org/students-and-educators

Joke

Q: What colors should you paint the sun and the wind?

A: The sun rose and the wind blue.

Power from
Weird Places

Mightier than the violent raging of the seas, mightier than
the breakers on the shore—the LORD above is mightier than these!
PSALM 93:4

A THOUSAND YEARS AGO, Vikings set up the first villages
in what became the nation of Iceland. Today Iceland is one of
the most efficient energy producers in the world. The type of power
used there comes directly from God's creation in the form of hydroelectric and geothermal power.

Hydroelectric power uses the flow of rivers to generate electricity. Water turns wheels attached to generators, which make electricity by turning big magnets. Sometimes people dam up rivers
to make hydroelectric plants, which drive water through rotating
engines to make electricity. Iceland has many dramatic rivers and
spectacular waterfalls, and they're put to good use: they power four-
fifths of the nation's energy needs.

Another kind of energy comes from heat within the Earth. It's
called geothermal energy (*geo* for "Earth," and *thermal* for "heat").
Volcanic places like Hawaii and Kenya tap into Earth's heat to
warm water and make steam for electricity. But when it comes to
geothermal power, Iceland is king. This volcanic island uses its
underground heat to produce over 20 percent of its power. Four out
of five homes in Iceland are geothermally heated. Iceland's goal for
the future is to be a completely fossil fuel–free country—for their
cars as well as for their cities' power

 Connection

There's a lot of power in the rivers of the world and in the rocks beneath us. When the people of Israel wandered in the desert, the Lord told Moses to strike a dry rock with his staff to get water for the people. "Moses struck the rock as he was told, and water gushed out" (Exodus 17:6). God's life-giving power is sometimes just beyond what we can see or touch, but he is always beside us, ready to help with his unseen power if we will only ask. Just as the Icelanders harness the hidden power under their feet, we can tap into God's invisible power through Jesus.

 What Can I Do?

Reduce your use of energy. An easy way to save energy—and money—is to have your parents turn your thermostat down a little in the winter and up a little in the summer. You can save 3 percent of your energy bill for each degree you turn your heat down in the winter and between 3 and 4 percent for each degree you turn your air conditioner thermostat up in the summer.

 **Fun Fact**

People have been using waterwheels for over 2,000 years. The ancient Greeks used waterwheels to operate grinding machines, which crushed wheat into flour. Other waterwheels pulled rope tied to big carts. Today's hydroelectric plants use the same kind of technology in new ways.

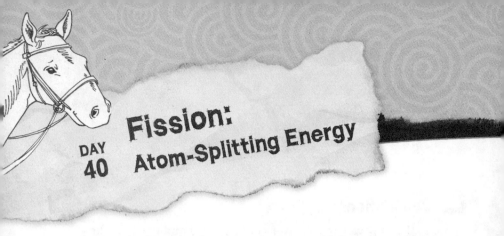

Fission: Atom-Splitting Energy

A prudent person foresees danger and takes precautions.
PROVERBS 22:3

MOST ELECTRICITY in the United States comes from coal-burning power plants. Heat from burning coal boils water into steam. The steam turns rotating engines called turbines, which spin magnets to create electricity. Nuclear plants don't use coal fire to heat water; instead, they heat water with a process called fission, using radioactive uranium fuel. In fission, a uranium atom splits into two smaller atoms. This split gives off heat. The nuclear plant uses the heat it produces just like a coal plant does—to provide power for things like charging your cell phone, toasting your bread, and playing your movies.

Fans of nuclear power point out that it makes less air pollution than other types of power plants and uses far fewer natural resources. A pellet of nuclear fuel the size of a AAA battery makes as much power as two tons of coal or six barrels of oil. But there's a drawback to nuclear power: radioactive fuel is dangerous. Used uranium is sealed in metal containers so it won't leak into our soil or rivers, but it will be deadly for centuries.

Nuclear plants have many safeguards to make sure nothing goes wrong, but sometimes even the best designs fail. The most famous nuclear accident happened in a Soviet plant called Chernobyl, in what is now Ukraine. On the morning of April 26, 1986, a test on the reactor went wrong because of an old design and people who were not properly trained. An explosion leaked radiation into the air, some of it reaching all the way to Europe. At least 56 people died soon after, and perhaps 4,000 died from cancer and other radiation-related diseases over the next few years. The radiation also sickened wildlife and fish.

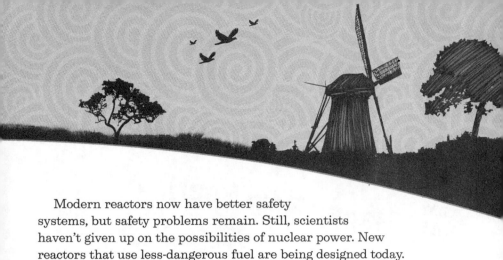

Modern reactors now have better safety systems, but safety problems remain. Still, scientists haven't given up on the possibilities of nuclear power. New reactors that use less-dangerous fuel are being designed today.

Connection

In all areas of technology and science, God expects his people to be responsible with the things they invent. The Bible says, "'Everything is permissible'—but not everything is beneficial. . . . Nobody should seek his own good, but the good of others" (1 Corinthians 10:23-24, NIV). God wants us to be careful with our decisions, and he wants us to ask for his wisdom about those things too.

What Can I Do?

Reflect on these questions. Is nuclear power a good thing? Does its efficient, clean energy outweigh its dangers? These are not easy questions. What do you think? Here are a few Web sites you can look at if you'd like to find out more information about this topic:

> http://www.eia.doe.gov/kids/energyfacts/sources/non-renewable/
> nuclear.html
> http://www.energy4me.org/sources/nuclear/index.htm

Factoid

As of 2009, nuclear power provides 15 percent of the world's electricity. There are 436 commercial nuclear power plants operating in 31 countries. The United States is home to 66 of these plants.

Happy New Year!

The people who walk in darkness
will see a great light.
ISAIAH 9:2

EVERY YEAR ON December 31, New York City's Times Square
has a big New Year's Eve celebration. As happy crowds count
down the seconds to the New Year, a gigantic ball slowly drops. Just
across the street, one of the largest billboards in the world shines
down with colorful lights. Instead of plugging into New York's typical electricity source, this 35,000-pound sign advertising the Ricoh
Americas Corporation has recently gone green.

The billboard is now powered by 45 solar panels and four rotating wind turbines. Batteries save the solar and wind energy from
that day for use at night. By using these alternate types of power,
the company saves $12,000 to $15,000 in energy costs every month.
That's a lot of electricity! In fact, the sign keeps 18 tons of carbon
out of the environment each month. It's just another way that
people are being creative about saving energy.

Connection

Every year we celebrate the coming of the New Year. It's a time to think about the past year—both good things we have accomplished and things that didn't go as planned. Sometimes as we look back over the year, we realize we haven't cared for God's world as he instructed in the days of Eden. But the New Year is a reminder that God gives second chances . . . and new beginnings. David, who wrote Psalm 145, knew this when he said, "The LORD is merciful and compassionate, slow to get angry and filled with unfailing love" (verse 8).

 What Can I Do?

Reflect *on the God of second chances.* Can you think of a time when God gave you a second chance—a chance to make something right? What happened?

Relay *your thoughts to God.* "Lord, thank you for being a God of second chances. Sometimes I think bad thoughts about others or tell little lies or treat people unkindly. But you are always there, always ready to forgive me and help me get a new beginning. God, you are awesome! Thank you for loving me."

Amazing Fact

If we could harness the sunlight energy that falls on the Earth in just one hour, it could provide all the energy the whole world would need for a year.

DAY 42 Energy from Moonbeams

*I look at the night sky and see the work of your fingers—
the moon and the stars you set in place.*
PSALM 8:3

UP IN SPACE, where there is no atmosphere, solar energy is eight times as powerful as it is here on Earth. Scientists are figuring out how to build large energy-grabbing satellites high above our planet. The satellites would beam the power down to stations on Earth. These orbiting power plants would be high enough that they would rarely pass into the Earth's shadow. In Japan, plans are underway to build a small satellite within the next few years to show that the technology really works. India is interested in the idea of beaming energy to remote villages that currently don't have normal electricity.

Building large structures in orbit is a difficult task. Some engineers think it would be easier to construct solar stations on the moon, where gravity would help astronauts in the building process. Many countries are interested in setting up outposts on the moon, and if they do, it will be much cheaper to build solar power stations on the moon than in Earth's orbit. Perhaps one day we will get our energy from solar station moonbeams!

 Connection

Beaming solar energy is just one possibility scientists are trying to figure out. We don't know what will work and what won't. All we can do is try many different creative ideas. One thing we do know about the future is that God will be there—he already has it planned out. God has plans for your future too! He says, "I know the plans I have for you . . . plans to prosper you and not to harm you, plans to give you hope and a future" (Jeremiah 29:11, NIV).

What Can I Do?

Reflect *on new ideas.* Most science museums have solar-powered toys and experiments you can try. You can buy solar-powered toys at the following Web sites:

    http://store.sundancesolar.com/soledkitandm.html
    http://www.fatbraintoys.com/toys/toy_categories/science_nature/
        electricity_solar_power/index.cfm
    http://www.crystalbay.net/solarvillage/solar-toys.html

Out-of-This-World Fact

The solar panels on the International Space Station take up more than an acre!

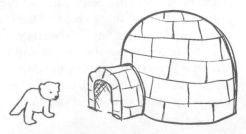

Fusion: Atom-Joining Energy

When you walk through the fire of oppression,
you will not be burned up; the flames will not consume you.
For I am the LORD, your God.
ISAIAH 43:2-3

EVERY BIT OF energy on the Earth's surface comes from the sun. The oil, coal, and wood we burn come from plants that got their energy from sunlight. Even animals are "solar powered," because they eat sunlight-energized plants . . . or other animals. Sunlight powers solar panels and drives the winds. But what powers the sun?

The sun, our nearest star, burns with nuclear fusion. Fusion is different from fission (see day #40). In nuclear fission, which is what happens in nuclear power plants, energy comes from splitting one atom into two. But in fusion, two atoms join together to form one larger atom. This is exactly what happens inside the sun and other stars, and also in nuclear bomb explosions.

It takes a lot of pressure and heat to make fusion happen, and that's the problem scientists are trying to solve in order to re-create solar power. To make fusion work, they need to heat the nuclear fuel to six times as hot as the sun's surface. At that temperature, the fuel would burn right through the strongest metal. So instead of using metal, scientists are trying to design ways to hold the nuclear reaction in a floating ball with lasers or strong magnetic fields.

The really cool thing about all this hot energy is that once it gets going, it makes far more energy than any other type of power. Fuel for fusion is less dangerous and more plentiful than fuel for fission reactors. And unlike the dangerous leftovers of fission, when nuclear fusion burns fuel, the leftovers are not radioactive. Fusion may solve many of the problems with today's nuclear energy.

Connection

Fusion requires a lot of heat and pressure, but once it gets going, it provides a lot of power. Sometimes, we feel pressure and heat from life's hard times. But in the end, God brings us through our difficulties. In Isaiah 43:2-3, we find God's promise to take care of us even in the middle of tough times.

What Can I Do?

React *wisely to tough times.* Sometimes God uses the tough times in our lives to make us into the people he wants us to be and to help us trust him more. The next time you face something difficult, ask God for help and be ready for him to change you for the better.

Interesting Fact

Power companies in the United States, Russia, Europe, China, Korea, India, and Japan have plans to build a fusion reactor called the International Thermonuclear Experimental Reactor (ITER) in Cadarache, France. Their goal is to prove that fusion can be used to make electricity.

News Flash

Researchers at the Naval Warfare Systems Center in San Diego, California, are close to inventing a process called "cold fusion," which may provide a safer and more efficient way of creating fusion energy.

DAY 44 Helium-3: More than Just a Funny Voice

God made two great lights—the larger one to govern the day,
and the smaller one to govern the night.
GENESIS 1:16

WHEN YOU FILL a birthday balloon with helium gas, it floats.
That's because helium is lighter, or less dense, than the air
around it. If you take a big whiff of it, your voice will sound like
SpongeBob. But helium floats around in the atmosphere, and we
breathe in tiny amounts of it all the time.

But there is another kind of helium that's a little different,
and that difference may be very important. This helium is called
helium-3, and it's a hot topic in science today. Researchers believe
that helium-3 can be used to create a clean and less dangerous
kind of nuclear fusion. Unlike other fuels used in nuclear reac-
tions (like plutonium), helium-3 is not radioactive, making it much
safer to store. But there's a problem: helium-3 is incredibly rare on
the Earth. However, there's a place nearby that may be a helium-3
shopping center: the moon. The surface of the moon is constantly
bombarded by solar wind, and that solar wind carries helium-3.
Scientists estimate that there are a million tons of helium-3 sitting
around on the moon—enough to power our world for thousands
of years.

Harrison Schmitt, a geologist and an astronaut on *Apollo 17*,
says that one space shuttle full of helium-3 (about 25 tons) could
power the entire United States for a year. It is hoped that future
astronauts can mine the soil of the moon for helium-3 to power
safe, clean fusion reactors here at home.

Connection

Because of his great love for us, God has made his creation to
provide us with things we need to take care of ourselves and his
world. Even though we don't often think about it, the moon is one
gift God has given us. He made it to "govern the night," and someday it may even help us power our homes!

What Can I Do?

Relay your thoughts to God. "God, you have given us all we need to
live a good life. Every good thing we have—like food, shelter, protection, love, and life—are gifts from you. Thank you!"

Interesting Fact

India's satellite Chandrayaan-1 recently finished orbiting the moon.
Its mission was to search for helium-3. Based on the findings from
this satellite, in September 2009 scientists confirmed the presence
of helium-3 on the moon.

Catching the Energy Wave

I am the LORD your God,
who stirs up the sea, causing its waves to roar.
ISAIAH 51:15

IN 1799, the Girards (a father and son team) invented a device to capture energy from ocean waves. Although their invention was never built, people have been thinking about that idea ever since. The ocean's waves, and the rise and fall of its tides, provide a constant flow of energy. The trick is to figure out how to grab that energy for our homes and cities.

Scientists are working on three kinds of energy from the ocean:

1. **Wave energy**: Off the coast of Portugal, huge orange metal tubes bob in the water. As they do, they move up and down like an old-fashioned hand pump, forcing seawater through power generators. If all goes well, Portugal plans to buy 28 more of these tubes—enough to power 15,000 homes. Other engineers are designing buoys that bob along in waves to make electricity.

2. **Energy from tides**: Twice each day, the ocean level rises and falls as the tide comes in and goes out. Engineers in France have built a special dam that allows the incoming tide to fill a reservoir. When the tide begins to go back out, the dam is closed off. Once the ocean is at its lowest point, the dam is opened and the water flows back into the sea through hydroelectric power plants. The plant generates enough electricity to power 240,000 homes in France. Other countries are building similar plants to harness the power of the ocean's tides.

3. **Energy from temperature**: Another promising idea is to use the difference in ocean temperatures to generate power. Ocean water is warm at the surface and cold far below. OTEC (which stands

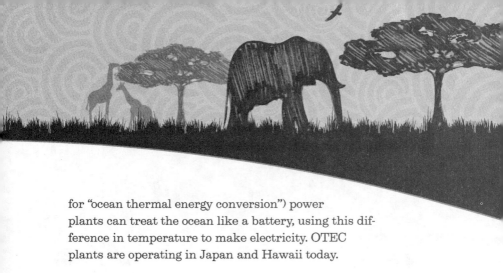

for "ocean thermal energy conversion") power plants can treat the ocean like a battery, using this difference in temperature to make electricity. OTEC plants are operating in Japan and Hawaii today.

Connection

God has given us plenty of power all around, including in the wind, sunlight, and waves. Sometimes the power of his creation can be scary, but Jesus is even more powerful than the waves in the ocean. We see this in Matthew 8:26-27, when Jesus was in a storm-tossed boat with his disciples: "He got up and rebuked the wind and waves, and suddenly there was a great calm. The disciples were amazed. 'Who is this man?' they asked. 'Even the winds and waves obey him!'"

What Can I Do?

Relay your thoughts to God. "Lord, your creation is so powerful. It reminds me of the greater power that you have. I hear your voice in the thunderstorm and feel your strength in the wind and waves. Thank you that your power comes to us in love. Thank you that your power changes our lives!"

Fun Fact

The power tubes in Portugal's ocean look like 450-foot-long orange snakes. The company that makes them, Pelamis, is named after a mythical Greek sea serpent.

Magnets of the Giants

We now have this light shining in our hearts, but we ourselves
are like fragile clay jars containing this great treasure. This makes
it clear that our great power is from God, not from ourselves.
2 CORINTHIANS 4:7

PLANET EARTH has a molten iron core that acts like a gigantic
magnet. Invisible magnetic lines flow around the world in big
curves that shoot out of one pole, stretch into space, and fall back
into the other pole. These lines look like the lines on a pumpkin,
with the North Pole being the stem. God has placed the magnetic
field around Earth to shield us from radiation that comes from
deep space and from the sun.

Our protective planetary magnet puts out a lot of energy. One
way to tap into that juice is by the use of space tethers. A space
tether is a wire that is many miles long. Spacecraft can unroll the
tether to cross those invisible magnetic lines. One end must be
near the Earth, and the other must be pointing away. As the tether
circles the Earth and passes through the magnetic lines, the energy
from inside our planet sets up an electrical current along the
tether. Scientists are designing ways to beam that power to Earth
in microwaves. Microwaves are the same type of energy used to
cook food in microwave ovens, but they can also beam messages or
power to another location.

The United States and other countries have experimented with
space tethers. In 1996, NASA orbited a tether that was 12 miles
long (or 20,000 meters), which generated a 3,500-volt current. Japan,
Europe, and the U.S. Naval Observatory are all working on space
tether projects. One day some of our power may come from giant
strings in the sky.

Connection

Our planet looks like a solid ball of rock and water on the outside, but amazing things are happening deep inside of it. The power that comes from the Earth's core is something we can't see, but it gives us important protection. Today's Bible passage from 2 Corinthians tells how God's protective Spirit lives within all of his children, no matter what they look like on the outside. Tall and short, old and young, from every country and race—all people who follow Christ have God's powerful Spirit inside, like a shield of protection and power.

What Can I Do?

Rethink *magnets.* The Earth's magnetic fields can be sensed by a compass. The needle on a compass always points to the north, lining up along the Earth's invisible magnetic lines. You can make a compass of your own. Here's how:

You will need a glass bowl of water, a pin, a cork, and a magnet.

1. Hold the pin firmly on one end and scrape the magnet from the bottom to the top of the pin.
2. Lift the magnet off the pin and bring it back down to the bottom, scraping the pin from the bottom to the top again (you must take the magnet away from the pin each time). Scrape the pin this way about 20 times.
3. Carefully push the pin through the top of the cork.
4. Lay the cork on the surface of the water in the bowl. The pin will point toward Earth's magnetic north pole!

Hint: You'll need to do this experiment far away from any telephones or TVs, as these devices have magnets in them and might pull the pin toward them.

Wild Experiences

All the animals of the forest are mine. . . . Every bird
on the mountains, and all the animals of the field are mine.
PSALM 50:10-11

PEOPLE AND WILD ANIMALS are living too close for comfort these days. Animals that used to live in remote areas are showing up in suburbs and cities. There are two main reasons for this: One is lack of food. The other is loss of habitat. If it can't find enough food, a hungry bear may wander into town looking for calories. Trash cans are easy pickings, and once the bear discovers this, it may decide that's the only way to go! If a deer population grows too big for the ecosystem to provide food for, many of the deer will wander down the mountain to nibble on backyard trees and bushes.

Loss of animal habitat is the other main problem. An animal's habitat is its natural home that gives it food and shelter. As our human population grows, and houses and businesses spread farther out into wilderness areas, animals lose their hunting grounds.

Jokes

Q: What did the umpire say when the little skunk came up to bat?
A: "Three stripes and you're out!"

Q: What do you get when you cross a skunk with a teddy bear?
A: Winnie the Pew!

 Connection

In the Garden of Eden, people and animals got along just fine, and in heaven we'll live in peace with all the animals there. Isaiah 11:6 tells us that one day in the future, "the wolf and the lamb will live together; the leopard will lie down with the baby goat. The calf and the yearling will be safe with the lion, and a little child will lead them all." But for now, in our fallen world, there will always be conflict between people and wild animals.

 **What Can I Do?**

Respect wildlife.

- Don't approach wild animals you see in your backyard or in the park. They may look cute and friendly, but they are still wild. They may attack you if they feel threatened.
- Don't pet or feed wild animals. This causes them to lose their fear of humans and may cause them to become aggressive.
- If you have raccoons living in your chimney, foxes denning under your house, or skunks making you hold your nose, you can find out how to get rid of them safely and humanely by logging on to http://www.wikihow.com/Get-Rid-of-Raccoons.

People can tame all kinds of animals, birds, reptiles, and fish, but no one can tame the tongue. It is restless and evil, full of deadly poison. Sometimes it praises our Lord and Father, and sometimes it curses those who have been made in the image of God.
JAMES 3:7-9

CANADA GEESE ARE beautiful birds that travel from Canada south to the United States each winter. They were hunted by people for food until their numbers became dangerously low and the government declared them a protected species, making it illegal to injure a Canada goose or damage its eggs. But now they're back . . . with a vengeance. Many Canada geese no longer migrate—instead, they camp out in the United States year-round.

Nowadays geese have few natural predators. Man-made lakes and ponds attract them to areas they normally wouldn't migrate to. Golf courses, apartment complexes, and parks are full of these birds. They are becoming pests: Nasty bacteria lurk in their poop. They pull up the grass with their beaks. They can be very aggressive to humans, especially when they think their goslings are in danger. They have been known to bite people and attack them with their wings.

All this does not make for a very fun time at the park or golf course. In the past few years, many golf courses have started using border collies to herd the geese and send them on their way. The collies keep the birds on the run or in the water until the geese give up and fly away. The birds then move on to lakes and ponds in less populated areas, and everyone is much happier.

♻️ Connection

As difficult as it is to control animals like Canada geese, James 3 says it's even more difficult to tame our tongues. Sometimes what comes out of our mouths is prayer or worship, and sometimes it's mean comments or complaints. But just like the collies help to keep the goose population under control, the Holy Spirit can help us keep our tongues in line.

What Can I Do?

Relay your thoughts to God. "Lord, whenever I am upset about something, help me to pause and choose my words carefully instead of expressing my anger through my language. Help me to tame my tongue."

Gross Fact

One adult Canada goose puts out two to four pounds of goose poop every day!

Joke

Q: What do you get when you cross a dog with a football player?

A: A golden receiver.

Monkeying Around

> You . . . are no longer strangers and foreigners.
> You are citizens along with all of God's holy people.
> You are members of God's family.
> EPHESIANS 2:19

UNLESS YOU DON'T MIND close encounters with feisty monkeys, you might want to think twice before moving to New Delhi, India. Thousands of hungry rhesus monkeys wander the city, looking for food. Some of them are "lab monkeys" that were abandoned after being used for experiments. The monkeys are aggressive, and they often attack and bite people. They break into homes and businesses. They've even broken into a police station and the Ministry of Defense offices, where they ripped up top-secret documents!

The city has brought in langur monkeys for use as "guard dogs" to chase off the smaller rhesus monkeys. But the langur monkeys are fierce and need to be kept on chains. The city also traps as many monkeys as it can and keeps them in cages. City officials would like to release the monkeys back into forests in nearby states, but most of the states don't want them. They say they already have monkey problems of their own.

People and wild animals can be a dangerous mix. The rhesus monkeys of New Delhi behave very badly. But the reason they act like this is because they are trying to survive in a new and unfamiliar environment. While they are at home in the jungle, they are aliens and outcasts in the city.

 Connection

Like the monkeys in the city of New Delhi, sometimes we might feel like we don't belong. When we move to a new neighborhood or start at a new school, it can be hard to fit in. But God loves us and has given us a place to fit into his family. Whenever you're feeling left out, reread Ephesians 2:19 as a reminder that you *do* belong.

 What Can I Do?

Reflect on these questions: Have you ever felt alone and afraid in a new place? How did God help you?

Startling Fact

There are reports of a gang of monkeys in Thailand that wait outside a convenience store until kids come out with Slurpees. Then the monkeys run up to the kids, screeching and making faces. The startled kids drop their Slurpees and run away, and then the monkeys carry off the drinks for themselves.

Jokes

Q: How do you get a one-armed monkey out of a tree?
A: You wave at him.

Q: Where does a monkey go if he loses his tail?
A: The retail store.

Close Encounters
of the Creature Kind

You send the darkness, and it becomes night,
when all the forest animals prowl about.
PSALM 104:20

ALMOST EVERY COMMUNITY has a story about forest animals moving into town. Raccoons nest in people's chimneys.
Bears raid garbage cans. Foxes move into neighborhoods. Coyotes
make snacks of small family pets.

Coyotes have also moved in to residential areas. These suburban
coyotes are losing their fear of people. This is a dangerous thing,
because it means the animals become aggressive. In 2009, there
were at least five coyote attacks on people in Denver. One victim
was a woman who was out walking her Labrador retriever.
Suddenly she and her dog were surrounded by three coyotes.
They attacked the dog. When the woman tried to protect her pet,
a coyote scratched and bit her. Both the woman and her dog had
to be hospitalized for their injuries.

Connection

God designed this world carefully so that everything would be in balance. He made the daytime, and he also planned for there to be darkness at night so animals can "prowl about" and find food, like it says in Psalm 104. When things in our world get out of balance, as they are with the coyote in some places, God gives us the important responsibility of helping to bring things back to order again.

 What Can I Do?

Reflect *on this dilemma.* When animals and people clash, it takes wisdom to know how to handle it. Everyone is upset about the aggressive coyotes that are starting to come into neighborhoods. Some people say the coyotes in suburban areas should be shot. Others say pets should be kept indoors and people should stay away from areas where coyotes could be. What do you think?

News Flash

Recently in Tucson, Arizona, some people spotted a mountain lion on a golf course. They called wildlife officials, who found the lion up in a tree. There were hundreds of rabbit bones scattered around the tree trunk. Apparently the lion had been living and hunting around the golf course for a long time. The officials tranquilized the lion and moved it to a remote area. They couldn't take the chance that the lion would attack a person.

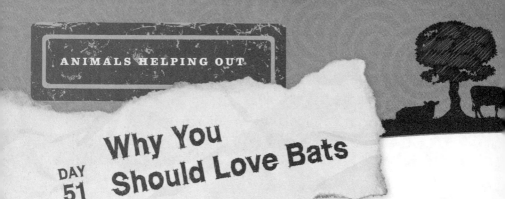

Why You Should Love Bats

Whatever is true, whatever is noble, whatever is right,
whatever is pure, whatever is lovely . . . think about
such things. . . . And the God of peace will be with you.
PHILIPPIANS 4:8-9, NIV

GOD MADE MOSQUITOES, but don't you sometimes wonder why he even had Noah bring them along in the ark? Mosquitoes are pesky. They can make summers miserable. Their bites can spread infections like the West Nile virus, malaria, and encephalitis (brain swelling), and they make millions of people sick every year.

If it seems like the mosquito population keeps getting larger, it's not just your imagination. Each year more dry areas are being used for farming and housing developments. People bring in water for these crops and lawns. This means there is more standing water than there used to be. And since mosquitoes lay their eggs in places with standing water, there are more mosquitoes. Yikes!

But thank goodness, God also made bats. Bats live almost everywhere in the world, and they love to eat flying insects. Some people have started using a foolproof way to get rid of the mosquitoes in their yards without using chemical bug sprays. They build or buy "bat boxes" to encourage bats to move in and eat the mosquitoes. Using one of God's creatures to restore nature's balance is a very cool idea.

 Connection

Sometimes our minds are full of buzzing thoughts that frustrate us and get us down, kind of like a bunch of mosquitoes. When that happens, you can use good thoughts to eat up those "mind mosquitoes" (negative thoughts). God's Word reminds us to think about "whatever is true . . . noble . . . right"—about good things.

 What Can I Do?

Reduce *your mosquito population.* Empty out standing water (like in birdbaths and plastic wading pools) every day to keep mosquitoes from laying eggs in it. If you are really feeling creative, you can also build some bat boxes! You might even have some small wooden boxes around the house that would work just fine. To find out more about bat boxes, go to http://batconservation.org/content/Bathouseimportance.html. (Warning: cats love to eat bats, so be sure your bat boxes are up high so the neighborhood felines can't get into them! Also, don't touch a bat that you find lying on the ground, since bats can be carriers of rabies.)

 News Flash

One bat can easily gobble up a thousand mosquitoes in a night.

Kudzu Catastrophe

Though we are overwhelmed by our sins,
you forgive them all.
PSALM 65:3

HERE IS ANOTHER story about people trying to make things better but causing disaster instead. But hopefully this story will have a happy ending. Kudzu is a fast-growing plant that was brought to America from Japan in 1876. People were encouraged to plant it in their yards as a shrub and also to grow it in fields to feed their horses and cattle. In the 1930s, government workers planted it to prevent soil erosion. But here in America, kudzu has no natural predators to keep it in check. Soon the kudzu vines spread everywhere and pushed out native plants. In the Southeastern states, where it is moist and warm, the kudzu grew . . . and grew . . . and grew. Now the battle is on. People burn the kudzu, then come in with skid loaders to dig out the roots. It's a very difficult job.

Chattanooga, Tennessee, is trying something new in "the battle of the kudzu." They've brought goats and llamas to the Missionary Ridge area east of town to graze on the kudzu and keep it under control. The llamas are also very aggressive toward predators, and this protects the goats. If this method of kudzu control works, more communities will have a new weapon in the battle of the kudzu.

 Connection

Sometimes we feel "overwhelmed by our sins," as Psalm 65 says. Like trying to get rid of the kudzu, it seems impossible. But God promises to forgive us and remove all the sin from our lives. Second Chronicles 20:12 says, "We do not know what to do, but our eyes are upon you" (NIV). We can trust God to show us how to overcome mistakes we have made.

 What Can I Do?

Relay your thoughts to God. Can you think of a mistake you have made that God helped you undo? Thank him for the times he has forgiven you. Is there anything in your life that is overwhelming you right now? You can ask for his help with that, too.

 Amazing Fact

A kudzu plant can grow 12 inches per day. Kudzu will completely cover anything in its path: houses, trees, and telephone poles.

Dolphins to the Rescue

DAY 53

Speak to the earth, and it will instruct you. Let the fish
in the sea speak to you. . . . For the life of every living thing
is in his hand, and the breath of every human being.
JOB 12:8, 10

THERE ARE MANY true accounts of dolphins helping save
swimmers in trouble. Here are two of them. In 2000, a
14-year-old boy fell off his father's boat near the coast of Italy. He
didn't know how to swim, and he was drowning. A dolphin swam
up to him and nudged him to the surface of the water. The boy
grabbed on to the dolphin. It towed him back to his father's boat.
When they were close enough, the boy's father was able to reach
down and pull the boy back into the boat.

In 2004, four lifeguards went on a training swim off the coast
of New Zealand. Suddenly a pod of dolphins swam up to them
and began swimming in a tight circle around them, slapping their
tails. The swimmers were scared and confused. They thought the
dolphins were being aggressive toward them—maybe to protect a
baby dolphin nearby. One of the lifeguards managed to swim away
from the circling dolphins. He looked down into the water . . . and
saw a great white shark under the surface! He realized the dolphins
were probably creating a "confusion screen" to protect the group of
swimmers from a shark attack. When a rescue boat came by, the
shark swam away. The dolphins stayed near the humans until they
were safely ashore.

Connection

Job 12:8, 10 tells us that nature reflects its maker. "Speak to the earth, and it will instruct you. Let the fish in the sea speak to you. . . . For the life of every living thing is in his hand, and the breath of every human being." God helps us and protects us, sometimes in unexpected and miraculous ways. David, who wrote many of the psalms, knew this. He said, "Protect me from those who have come to destroy me. . . . See what is happening and help me!" (Psalm 59:1, 4).

What Can I Do?

Reflect on what God has done. Can you think of a time when God helped you in a surprising way? Take a moment to thank God for his help, and then tell someone about what he did for you!

☀ Fun Fact

Scientists consider dolphins some of the most intelligent animals in the world. Researchers are studying the language dolphins use to communicate with each other (mostly sounds and whistles) to try to learn more about these amazing creatures.

Joke

Q: Why did the dolphin cross the ocean?

A: To get to the other tide.

Dogs That Serve

If your gift is serving others, serve them well.
ROMANS 12:7

SINCE ANCIENT TIMES, people have used dogs for herding, protection, and companionship. In the last century or so, people have begun specially training dogs to help the disabled. These dogs give people with special needs the gift of safety, emotional security, and independence.

Service Dogs: On the morning of September 11, 2001, a man who was blind was working in his office at the World Trade Center. As always, his guide dog was with him. Suddenly a huge explosion shook the tower. The World Trade Center towers had been hit in terrorist attacks! The man's dog guided him through the smoke and flames, all the way down 71 flights of stairs. Because of the dog's help, the man made it out of the building to safety.

Service dogs also help people who are deaf and those in wheelchairs. In Colorado Springs, 14-year-old Veren Betzen is on the go with his service dog, Comet. Veren has cerebral palsy and is in a wheelchair. He has only limited use of his hands. Comet helps Veren by opening the refrigerator door for him, picking up things Veren drops, helping him get dressed, and going to school with him. Comet also helps Veren make friends. Students who might be nervous around Veren because he has trouble talking and moving come over to see the dog and end up talking to Veren. Comet recently lost one of his legs because of a disease, but this three-legged helper still goes everywhere with his master. Comet gives everyone around him a lot of joy.

Therapy dogs: In the 1950s, a doctor who worked with disturbed children found that the children made dramatic progress when he brought his dog to therapy for them to play with. Since that time,

therapy dogs have been trained to help physically, mentally, and emotionally disabled adults and children. A child who has trouble walking might work very hard to walk far enough to pet a friendly dog nearby. An elderly person in a nursing home who is feeling depressed may smile and talk to a visiting therapy dog.

Connection

Service dogs and therapy dogs have an amazing ability to serve people who need their help and care. Just as these animals serve people, God calls us to serve others. He tells us to "serve one another in love" (Galatians 5:13). How can you serve someone today?

What Can I Do?

Reconsider *what dogs can do.* Dogs don't just make great pets! Here are a couple of things to consider about working dogs:

- Don't pet a service dog while he is working. You don't want to distract the dog from doing its job.
- If you and your family own a gentle, friendly dog, you can go to special training classes and then take your pet to visit people in hospitals and nursing homes.

Joke

Q: What kind of dog likes baths?

A: A shampoodle.

DAY 55 Horse Power

Let your gentleness be evident to all.
PHILIPPIANS 4:5, NIV

MAI WISDOM OF Sterling, Colorado, has loved horses all her life. She wanted to share the special joy of horseback riding with others. So she and her friend started a nonprofit program that provides horses for disabled kids to ride. Several people donated calm, gentle horses to help. Programs like this can be found across the country.

When a horse and a human work together, there is often a special bond that develops. People have learned to use this connection to help those with disabilities. Therapeutic horseback riding can be used to help people with physical, mental, and emotional problems. It can make the hard work of therapy a little more fun for everybody involved.

Here's an example of how therapeutic riding can help a child with Down syndrome. A boy or girl with Down syndrome may have many mental and physical difficulties. Riding is a good challenge for the child's brain. The rider learns how to say the horse's name, give the horse commands, and name the horse's body parts and the words for the riding equipment: saddle, bridle, stirrups, etc. The rider also learns how to mount and dismount, and how to hold the reins to guide the horse. Riding gives the child confidence, better balance and coordination, and stronger muscles. It often improves walking and speech. Two people—the leader and the side walker—walk beside the horse, one on each side. They are there to help the child keep his or her balance and to coach the horse and the rider. The time spent with a horse can improve the child's health—in both mind and body.

Connection

Horses are extremely powerful animals, yet they are gentle with the people who are riding them, especially those who need extra care. God expects us to be gentle too. In today's verse from Philippians, we are told to be gentle to everyone. Think of ways you can be kind and patient with the people in your life, especially those who need extra attention.

 What Can I Do?

Reconsider *what horses can do.* Riding a horse can be good therapy for anyone, not just those with disabilities. Spending time on one of these beautiful animals is good exercise for the body and wonderful for the spirit.

Cool Web Site

Visit http://www.narha.org to find the therapeutic horseback riding center nearest to you.

Joke
Knock, knock.
Who's there?
Rhoda.
Rhoda who?
Rhoda horse yesterday; did you?

DAY 56

Animals in the Danger Zone

> You care for people and animals alike, O LORD.
> PSALM 36:6

GOD CARES FOR all his creatures, and he also wants us to take care of them. But some animals in the wild are becoming rare—and even extinct—very quickly. Pollution and forest clearing destroy many of the wilderness homes that God's creatures live in. These animals are dying out because they can no longer find food or a place to live, or because they are being hunted illegally. Sometimes they live in an area where there is war, which destroys their homes.

Some creatures are already long gone, but we can still learn from them. Extinct species remind us to take care of the animals we still have. Gorillas, tigers, blue whales, orangutans, Arabian oryx, condors, whooping cranes, and many other creatures are endangered. But it is not too late! With God's help, we can protect his creatures and the wilderness where they live.

♻ Connection

God used his mighty creativity to fill the world with more kinds of animals than we could ever imagine. And he cares for each thing he has made. Psalm 148:5 says, "Let every created thing give praise to the LORD, for he issued his command, and they came into being." We can thank God for creating every living thing—and for caring about each creature and person he has made.

 ## What Can I Do?

Reflect *on your role in creation.* What do you think God meant when he told us to rule over his creatures (see Genesis 1:28)? What's something you can do to make sure you're doing this job well?

Research *ways you can help.* Visit http://www.kidsplanet.org/ factsheets/map.html. This site gives lots of information about endangered animals and where they live. Organizations like Sierra Club (http://www.sierraclub.org) and the Nature Conservancy (http://www.nature.org) also work to preserve rare animals and their habitats.

☀ News Flash

Thanks to the hard work of many people, both the peregrine falcon and the gray whale have recently been taken off the endangered list.

PARADE OF TERMS

Near Threatened: These animals may be considered threatened in the near future. The manta ray is one of these.

Threatened: These species are at risk of becoming endangered soon. An example is the cheetah—there are about 12,000 worldwide.

Endangered: This refers to animals at risk of becoming extinct in the near future. The blue whale is endangered. There are only about 2,500 now, but their population is increasing slowly.

Critically Endangered: These animals are at extreme risk of becoming extinct in the immediate future. An example is the northern white rhino, with only 35 left in the wild.

Extinct in the Wild: Captive animals still survive, but there is no natural population left in the wild. One example is the South China Xiamen tiger (there are only about 20 left in zoos).

Extinct: The last member of the species has died or is presumed dead. An example is the dodo bird.

113

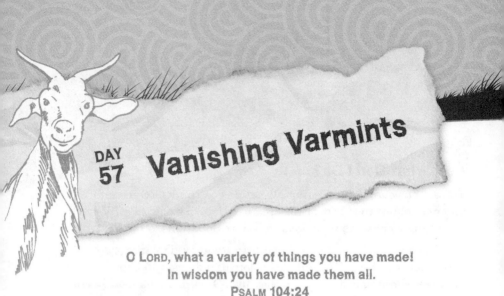

Vanishing Varmints

O LORD, what a variety of things you have made!
In wisdom you have made them all.
PSALM 104:24

IT'S THE CASE of the vanishing varmints! Many weird and sometimes woolly creatures have gone missing from the world. They are extinct . . . deceased . . . no longer kicking. Today we see reminders of the great mammals that lived around here in prehistoric times. The elephants today are similar to (but smaller than) the massive woolly mammoths—furry pachyderms that stood over twice as tall as a person and had tusks 14 feet long. In North America, camels used to gallop past herds of gigantic prehistoric bison, hunted by scary saber-toothed Smilodons.

There were even stranger beasties. The Eobasileus had three rows of rhino-like horns along the top of its head and two tusks jutting out from its lower jaw. The Indricotherium looked like a huge, short-necked giraffe. This giant creature weighed as much as four elephants! And speaking of elephants, there used to be dwarf elephants in southern Europe no bigger than a German shepherd!

Many of these mammals had heavy fur to keep them warm, as the world was colder back then. Glaciers covered most of North America, and summers were cool and short. When things warmed up and the glaciers melted, these exotic Ice Age mammals "melted" away too. Genesis makes it clear that God created new animals right up until the time of Adam and Eve. For some reason, God allowed some animals to be removed from the world. But as we study their bones and learn about their ancient habitats, even those creatures that are gone help us to marvel at the Creator of our world.

 Connection

God's creatures show us how creative he is. They show us his power, too. Psalm 104:24 puts it this way: "O LORD, what a variety of things you have made! In wisdom you have made them all. The earth is full of your creatures."

What Can I Do?

Reflect on God's creativity. Which of the Ice Age animals would you be most curious to see? What can these creatures tell you about who God is?

Review the past. Woolly mammoths and hadrosaurs are gone forever. But there are creatures around today that are in trouble, and you can help. In addition to joining groups that help animals (see day #56), you can do your part to keep the wilderness clean and healthy. After all, it's the animals' home, too!

Jokes

Q: What is shaggy, has a wand and huge wings, flies at night, and gives money to young woolly mammoths?
A: The tusk fairy.

Q: What do you get if you cross a woolly mammoth and a kangaroo?
A: Big holes all over the ice.

Dinosaurs: Mega and Mini

God made all sorts of wild animals, livestock, and small animals, each able to produce offspring of the same kind. And God saw that it was good.

GENESIS 1:25

DINOSAURS WERE THE largest creatures ever to live on the land. They were not mammals. They did not have fur (some of them had scales and some had feathers), and they laid eggs. Their skeletons were very much like those of birds, and they were probably warm-blooded.

God made dinosaurs in many shapes and sizes. They had horns, crests, crowns, and frills (shieldlike collars made of bone). God designed some dinosaurs to eat veggies and others to eat meat. Just as we see in the wilderness today, there were far more herbivores (plant eaters) than carnivores (meat eaters). Some of the most common herbivores were the hadrosaurs, which were duck-billed dinosaurs. These dinos had wide, flat bills just like those of ducks, but these "ducks" were as long as three cars! Some herbivores, like the Lambeosaurus and Corythosaurus, had beautiful crests on top of their heads. The Parasaurolophus had a long tube at the back of its head. Airways inside the tube probably helped this hadrosaur to make low, rumbling sounds to call other dinosaurs or warn enemies. There were many other plant-eating dinosaurs too, from the horned triceratops to the long-necked sauropods.

Meat-eating dinosaurs were built for speed and hunting. They had sharp, powerful claws and teeth. Dinosaurs like the Allosaurus had sharp claws for holding on to their dinner. Velociraptors had knife-sharp teeth that curved backward to help them grab a snack.

 Connection

Like the mammoths and saber-toothed cats, dinosaurs have shown us that God's creatures can sometimes disappear very quickly. The Bible says that our time here on earth is short too: "We are here for only a moment. . . . Our days on earth are like a passing shadow, gone so soon without a trace" (1 Chronicles 29:15). But if we know Jesus and live for him, we will spend all of eternity with him!

 What Can I Do?

Reflect on this question: What can we learn about taking care of God's world from the dinosaurs and other prehistoric creatures?

Joke

Q: What do you get when you cross a dinosaur with a termite?

A: Dynomite.

The Largest Land Mammal in the World

The king [Solomon] made a huge throne,
decorated with ivory and overlaid with fine gold.
1 KINGS 10:18

THE ELEPHANT IS the largest land mammal in the world. An African bull (male) elephant weighs as much as a truck. He stands 10 feet tall, eats 500 pounds of leaves and grass, and drinks about 30 gallons of water every day. Elephants live for about 65–70 years. An elephant is born helpless, and it needs constant care to survive. The baby nurses from its mother for five years and is gently guided and taught how to survive by the females in the herd.

The only mention of elephants in the Bible comes from 1 Kings, where ivory is called "elephant teeth" in the original language. The Assyrians hunted Asian elephants for their tusks during Bible times, and war elephants were used in ancient battles. Back then, elephants were the equivalent of tanks in modern warfare. Their thick hide protected them from arrows. The riders sat up high for a good view and ran the elephants through the opposing army's ranks, trampling the enemy's soldiers.

Joke

Q: Why are elephants no good at surfing the Internet?

A: Because they're scared of the mouse.

 Connection

Although elephants are powerful, they only use their full power when they have to. God has given us great power, but he wants us to use it in gentleness and wisdom. Some people lecture their friends or try to force them to agree, but you can show the same gentle spirit that the elephant has toward its young. God's Word says, "Be completely humble and gentle; be patient, bearing with one another in love" (Ephesians 4:2, NIV).

What Can I Do?

Rethink your purchases. Don't buy toys, jewelry, or anything else made of real ivory. If people stop buying things made from elephants, poachers (illegal hunters) will stop killing them. Here are a few other things to avoid at the store:

- **Coral jewelry**: Buy carefully. Some coral reefs are dying from overharvesting. Make sure any coral you buy has been imported with a CITES permit.
- **Cactus**: Find out where those prickly houseplants come from! Huge areas of cacti are being wiped out in Mexico and other wilderness areas through illegal trade. Make sure yours comes from a garden or commercial greenhouse.

News Flash

Millions of elephants used to live in Africa. Now that number has dropped to between 470,000 and 690,000. But these animals are protected, and their numbers are increasing. Asian elephants are officially considered to be endangered. There are only about 30,000 left in the wild.

Sumatran Tiger

We . . . live peaceful and quiet lives
marked by godliness and dignity.
1 TIMOTHY 2:2

SUMATRAN TIGERS ARE the smallest of the tiger family.
They are solitary and hunt at night. They need surprise on
their side, because they can run fast only for a short distance.
When Sumatran tigers go hunting, they fail 9 times out of 10. They
hate to climb trees, which is a good thing for apes like orangutans
and gibbons, which can hide from their predators up in treetops.
Sumatran tigers love to swim, and they easily catch fish and frogs.
They have even been seen swimming in the ocean, keeping cool
in the midst of their hot tropical climate. Male tigers mark their
"ownership" of areas by spraying urine, and their roars can be
heard a mile away. Tiger cubs are born helpless and stay with their
mother for two years, learning how to be successful hunters.

God gave these beautiful beasts stripes for camouflage.
Camouflage is a pattern that helps an animal blend into its
surroundings so it can hide. Sumatran tigers have black stripes,
and these stripes mimic the dark shadows in the jungle. Every tiger
has a slightly different pattern of stripes, like a fingerprint. Their
camouflage helps them to sneak up on their prey.

Connection

The stripes of the tiger make it one of a kind. No other creature has stripes quite like it. God has put "stripes" on his followers to set them apart too. As it says in today's verse, we are "marked by godliness and dignity." We are striped (marked) by traits or actions that make it obvious to the world that we are Christ followers. The marks of a Christian include a loving and kind spirit and a giving nature.

What Can I Do?

Reflect on these questions: Can you name some other "stripes" God gives us that set Christians apart from the rest of the world? Which ones do you need to work on? Which are your strengths?

News Flash

Sumatran tigers are an endangered species. There are only about 100 left in the wild.

Joke

Q: Would you rather have a tiger eat you or a lion?

A: I'd rather have the tiger eat the lion.

Whales and Other Olympic Swimmers

> God created great sea creatures and every living thing
> that scurries and swarms in the water. . . .
> And God saw that it was good.
> GENESIS 1:21

THEY SPLASH. They swim. Some of them even sing underwater! They are the mammals of the sea. Whales, dolphins,
and porpoises belong to a special mammal family called cetaceans.
They have smooth, rubbery skin and flippers to help them swim
well. Like all mammals, they breathe air. Cetaceans have a "blow
hole" on the top of their heads, which they breathe in and out of
while staying almost completely underwater. They have a layer of
fat called blubber that keeps them warm even in the coldest water.

Most whales are baleen whales. This means that they have a
comblike curtain, called baleen, in the front of their mouths. They
use this curtain to filter out other items so they can enjoy little
creatures called krill, which are similar to shrimp. Even though
baleen whales are some of God's most mega creatures, they eat tiny
stuff! The blue whale is the largest creature that has ever lived.
This baleen giant is as long as nine cars, weighs as much as 40 elephants, and has a heart the size of a Volkswagen Beetle. It is also
the rarest whale, and it is listed as endangered.

Over a hundred years ago, whales were hunted in all the world's
oceans, but whaling is now forbidden in the United States except
in the case of Inuit peoples. They take only what they need for
their society and traditions. Now that large fishing fleets have been
ordered to stop hunting whales, experts hope the whale population
will be able to increase.

 Connection

Our hearts have their own sort of baleen: the Holy Spirit. The Spirit helps us figure out the right thing to do and filter out things that get in the way of our walk with God, like gossip or selfishness. The Bible says, "Those who live in accordance with the Spirit have their minds set on what the Spirit desires" (Romans 8:5, NIV).

 **What Can I Do?**

Reflect *on new ideas.* Want to keep up on the latest about whales? Here are a few Web sites that keep tabs on our oceangoing friends:

http://www.whalewatch.com/kids

http://www.timeforkids.com/TFK/kids/news/
    story/0,28277,1902215,00.html

http://www.sciencedaily.com/news/plants_animals/
    dolphins_and_whales

News Flash

There's good news about blue whales! They have increased from a few hundred in the 1960s to a few thousand today.

Jokes

Q: How do you make a whale float?
A: Get a huge glass, a can of soda, two scoops of ice cream, and a whale.

Q: Why did the whale eat two ships loaded with potatoes?
A: Because no one can eat just one potato ship.

Not Your Average House Cats

There are three things that walk with stately stride—
no, four that strut about: the lion, king of animals,
who won't turn aside for anything. . . .
PROVERBS 30:29-30

LIONS ARE THE biggest hunters in the grasslands of Africa. They help keep nature in balance by killing off the sick and weak herbivores (plant eaters) so the herds don't get too big. Lions are the only members of the cat family that live in groups. There can be as many as 30 lions in these groups, called prides. Lionesses can have up to five cubs at a time, but usually they have a litter of two or three. Even though they grow up to be strong and powerful, lion cubs aren't born "ready to run." They are tiny, helpless, and blind when they are born, and they weigh less than two pounds.

The lionesses do almost all the hunting for the pride. The females in the pride help each other care for the cubs and take turns "babysitting" when the other females go off to hunt. They usually hunt at night as a group, sometimes stalking their prey for hours before attacking.

Although a number of their cousins are endangered or threatened, the good news is that African lions are not endangered. This is because wise people have created big wildlife reserves for them to live and hunt in. Things aren't so good for the Asian lions, however. They are endangered—there are only about 200 left in the wild.

 Connection

In the Bible, the mighty lion often symbolizes Christ. This idea is used because of his majestic power. Revelation 5:5 describes Christ as "the Lion of the tribe of Judah." The lion also symbolizes God's courageous justice. Ezekiel 1 talks about a lion-faced creature guarding God's throne.

 What Can I Do?

Relay your thoughts to God. "Thank you, Jesus, that you are so full of majestic power. Thank you for being strong and mighty, and more powerful than a lion!"

Factoid

Before the end of the last Ice Age, lions lived in North and South America. Today, their cousins the panthers still do!

Joke

Q: What do you get when you cross a parrot with a lion?

A: I don't know, but when it talks, you'd better listen carefully.

A Whooping Success Story

The wild animals honor me.
ISAIAH 43:20, NIV

ONE CREATURE NEARLY died out about 70 years ago, but people were able to save it. The graceful whooping cranes are the tallest birds in North America. Whooping cranes fly 5,400 miles each year, from their nesting grounds in Texas to the marshy wilderness of northern Canada. But in 1941, only 16 of the beautiful birds were left.

Conservationists in the United States and Canada sprang into action, protecting the rare birds' nesting grounds and taking some eggs so that they could start a protected captive flock. These chicks were then raised using crane puppets so that they did not see humans. In this way, the birds remained "wild." As the chicks grew, they were released to be with the only wild cranes left. This group of birds has now grown to almost 300. The cranes continue to journey each year from Texas to Canada and back again.

Another flock was started in Florida, and a third travels between Florida and Wisconsin. From a tiny flock of 16, humans have helped bring whooping cranes back from the brink of extinction. There are now over 350 wild cranes, with about 250 more in captivity. Many of the captive birds will one day be released into the wild.

Connection

All animals—including dinosaurs, birds, and mammals—bring glory to their Creator. God designed each one to have a special place in his world. From windblown deserts to soggy jungles, God's creatures jump, dash, fly, swim, and scamper. As beautiful as these creatures are, they are only a dim reflection of God's beauty. Think about these wonderful words in Revelation 5:13 (NIV): "I heard every creature in heaven and on earth and under the earth and on the sea, and all that is in them, singing: 'To him who sits on the throne and to the Lamb be praise and honor and glory and power, for ever and ever!'"

What Can I Do?

Reflect *on new ideas.* You can become a member of the International Crane Foundation, an organization that protects cranes worldwide. Take a look at their Web site: http://www.savingcranes.org/whoopingcrane.html.

Crazy Fact

Captive-raised whooping crane chicks had to learn to fly with the rest of the flock. To lead them, conservationists flew in one-man ultralight airplanes.

127

Modern-Day Noah's Arks

Pairs of every kind of bird, and every kind of animal, and every kind of small animal that scurries along the ground, will come to you to be kept alive.
GENESIS 6:20

THE BOOK OF GENESIS tells about when God saved the animals from a massive flood. He told Noah to take two of each kind of animal onto a huge boat called an ark. Today, many zoos throughout the world serve as modern Noah's arks, saving rare animals. Most zoos try to create environments similar to the places where the animals are from. One such place is San Diego Zoo's Wild Animal Park, where herds of rare and endangered creatures roam free in areas much like their homes in the wild. Giraffes mingle with herds of wildebeests, while rhinos wade in ponds next to flamingos and hippos.

Zoos create herds of rare animals by borrowing animals from other zoos to mate with theirs. The combination of diverse animals keeps the captive herds healthy. Eventually the creatures in the captive herds can be taught how to survive in the wilderness, and they are put back into the wild. Some successful programs have involved nearly extinct animals such as the Arabian oryx, the California condor, and the last true wild horses, Przewalski's horses.

But the battle is far from over for many of these creatures. In the 1980s and 1990s, several dozen oryx were set free into the wilderness of Oman, where they grew in numbers to a herd of 400. But poachers came in and killed most of the herd, and by 1999, only about 200 were still alive. Today their population has dwindled to a handful. Poaching continues to be a major reason for extinction of animals, but things are slowly improving. Now there are strong laws that discourage poachers from hunting rare animals, and much work is being done by rangers in African and Asian national parks to stop poachers and protect the animals.

 Connection

When God sent the Flood in Noah's time, God was careful to preserve the creatures, just two of each kind. God's creatures are important to him, and he gives us the opportunity to help take care of them too. An entire species can be helped when people start with just a handful of animals, as zoos have done with rare populations like the whooping crane and Arabian oryx.

 What Can I Do?

Reflect on God's world. Many zoos have Arabian oryx. Take time to visit a zoo near you to see these beautiful, rare creatures God made!

☀ **News Flash**

Good news! A new herd of Arabian oryx in Saudi Arabia doubled in size in a span of four years. In 2007, the United Arab Emirates released 100 Arabian oryx into the Abu Dhabi desert, and by 2012, another 500 will be released.

Joke

Q: What kind of lights were on the ark?

A: Floodlights.

DAY 65 Bottled Water Everywhere

Tune your ears to wisdom, and concentrate on understanding. . . .
Search for them as you would for silver;
seek them like hidden treasures.
PROVERBS 2:2, 4

ONE OF THE BIGGEST landfill cloggers here in the United States is the plastic water bottle. Americans go through more than 2.5 million of them *per hour*. Eight out of ten of these bottles end up in landfills every year. Can you guess how many years it takes these bottles to even *begin* to decompose? About 500 years! Some water bottle companies are using much thinner plastic for their water bottles to try to reduce waste. This helps the problem a little, but not much.

It is difficult for the plastic material in water bottles to be broken down and recycled into a material that can be used again. That's because different water bottle companies use different "recipes" for their plastic. It takes a lot of time and energy for recycling plants to sort out the different brands of bottles.

But there are other solutions—ones that don't require the help of water bottling companies or recycling plants. People were drinking water for many years before plastic was even invented. So maybe there are things our country can do—and you can do—to rewind the clock! Take a look on the next page for some ideas.

 Connection

As it says in today's verse from Proverbs, we should search for wisdom and view it as even more valuable than buried treasure. One benefit of wisdom is that it helps us change the way we live. Is there a plastic water bottle in your hand or in your pantry? Long after you are done with it, it will still be taking up space . . . virtually forever. Ask God to help you be wise with his creation.

 What Can I Do?

Reflect *on these questions:* Is it wise to keep buying and using plastic water bottles? Can you think of some things you can do instead?

Reuse *water bottles.* If you do only one thing in this book, this might be the most important: carry a refillable canteen or metal water bottle everywhere you go. Put your name on it to help you keep track of it. Think ahead and take your water bottle with you when you go to events. Then you won't have to buy a bottle for four dollars at the zoo or at a sports event. You'll be saving money *and* the environment.

Fun Fact

In July 2009, the Australian town of Bundanoon voted to be a water bottle–free town. Reusable bottles are sold to people, and they can refill these bottles with filtered water in shops and other public places for a small fee.

Glass Act

Now we see things imperfectly, like puzzling reflections in a mirror, but then we will see everything with perfect clarity. All that I know now is partial and incomplete, but then I will know everything completely, just as God now knows me completely.
1 CORINTHIANS 13:12

GLASS IS A wonderful invention. It can be used to make everything from lightbulbs to mirrors to windows. Glass is made in factories by machines that melt together sand, soda ash, and lime. The hot glass is formed into shapes. Then, as it cools, it hardens. Glass can be recycled over and over again, which is great.

But there's one drawback: the three things glass is made of (sand, soda ash, and lime) are nonrenewable resources. When they get used up, they'll be gone for good. There is still hope for glass though (see the suggestions below under "What Can I Do?").

Factoid

Q: How long does it take for a glass bottle to decompose back into dirt?

A: Hundreds of thousands of years.

♻ Connection

Glass is good for making all sorts of household objects, and one of those is a mirror. Mirrors aren't perfect, of course. Fun-house mirrors are warped to make us look tall and skinny or short and wide. Even a normal mirror doesn't show things exactly as they are. The Bible says that life on Earth is like that. We sometimes wonder what God is up to or why certain things happen. We can't see God's plan clearly yet—it's as if we are looking at "puzzling reflections in a mirror." But when we get to heaven and see Jesus face-to-face someday, things will become clear. "Now we see things imperfectly . . . but then we will see everything with perfect clarity" (1 Corinthians 13:12). So when life is frustrating, be patient! One day God will make all things clear to you.

 What Can I Do?

Recycle. Even though the things that make up glass are nonrenewable, glass itself is renewable. We can recycle glass to be used over and over (but only if it's clear, brown, or green). Just take off the lid and rinse out the bottle or jar, and it's ready to be recycled. You don't even have to peel off the label (yea!).

Reuse. Use glass bottles and jars in new ways: an empty jar can hold pennies, shells, pens, or pencils. An empty bottle can make a nice vase for flowers.

Regift. You can donate glass vases and mirrors to secondhand stores or donation centers so they can be used again. Used eyeglasses can be donated and reused by people who can't afford them—both in the United States and in other countries.

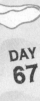

Here a Can, There a Can, Everywhere a Soda Can

DAY 67

> It is a land where food is plentiful and nothing is lacking.
> It is a land where iron is as common as stone,
> and copper is abundant in the hills.
> DEUTERONOMY 8:9

DID YOU KNOW that mountains and hills are full of metal? Over the years, people have figured out ways to get that metal out and use it to make things. It works like this: rocks are dug up from the ground and then heated and melted to remove the metal. The two kinds of metal we use most are aluminum and steel.

Aluminum is often used for food cans, soda cans, and cooking pans. Steel is used to make cars, planes, buildings, and bridges. But just like fossil fuels (see day #27 and day #31), metal is made from nonrenewable resources. When we use up all the rocks with metal in them, that's it. There isn't any more. That's why recycling is so important!

Joke

Q: What is our world's biggest problem: ignorance or apathy?

A: I don't know, and I don't care.

 Connection

The verse in Deuteronomy is talking about the Promised Land, which was the country God gave to his special people, the Israelites, after they were set free from slavery in Egypt. The land God has given us today is full of good resources too, but these won't last forever. The good news is that God himself is a "renewable resource." He will never get used up; we will never run out of him. He will give us all the energy and power we need to live life. He gives us this promise: "Be sure of this: I am with you always, even to the end of the age" (Matthew 28:20).

 What Can I Do?

Recycle your aluminum. It's never been easier to send your used soda cans to be recycled. Most schools have recycling containers for cans and bottles. Some lunchrooms even have can crushers attached to the wall. These are used to squish soda cans flat before they're put into the recycling bin.

 Amazing Fact

It takes less energy to make metal items from recycled materials than it does to make new items. The hard work of getting the metal out of the rock has already been done, so the metal just needs to be melted down and reshaped.

The Mystery of the Triangles

He has showed you, O man, what is good.
And what does the LORD require of you?
To act justly and to love mercy and
to walk humbly with your God.
MICAH 6:8, NIV

SEVEN DIFFERENT TYPES of plastic can be recycled. Each one has its own symbol. The first time you saw these triangles on the bottom of your plastic containers and food bags, you might have thought they looked like Egyptian hieroglyphics. But there's a key to crack this code! There are two types of plastic that are most often recycled. The first has a triangle with a number one inside it and "PET" or "PETE" under it. *PET* stands for polyethylene terephthalate, if you must know! The second has a triangle with a number two inside it and "HDPE" (high-density polyethylene) under it.

Recycled PET plastic (#1) is melted down and pulled into long, thin fiber strands. Then it's made into carpets, T-shirts, fleece jackets, and shopping bags. HDPE (#2) is made into plastic lumber and Tyvek mailing envelopes.

Plastics labeled #3–5 have a lower rate of recyclability than #1 and #2. Plastic labeled #3 includes items such as plastic pipes, shower curtains, medical tubing, and vinyl dashboards. Plastic with a #4 includes grocery and sandwich bags, and #5 includes containers such as Tupperware. This doesn't mean you can't recycle them, but they take more time and energy to make into new recycled items. This is why it's good to reuse plastic bags as many times as possible.

Plastic #6 is polystyrene, which is what disposable coffee cups, plastic silverware, meat trays, and packing peanuts are made of. Now #6 is being accepted by many recycling plants because it can be made into recording tape and foam insulation.

 Connection

Today's verse says that God wants us to "act justly." This means that we do what is fair and right in the way we treat other people, animals, and the environment. One way we can act justly is to take responsibility for the stuff we use—and the stuff we get rid of. This verse also instructs us to "walk humbly" with God. When we think about how our actions affect other people and our world, we are taking a step in the direction of humility.

 **What Can I Do?**

Review your plastic. Take a minute to decipher the hieroglyphics on your plastic bottles. Also, find out which numbers of plastic your local recycling center will accept.

Recycle. It's pretty simple these days to recycle your plastic. Lots of communities have recycling centers, and most trash collection companies offer curbside recycling services.

Joke

> Teacher: Tommy, give me an example of a collective noun.
>
> Tommy: Garbage can.

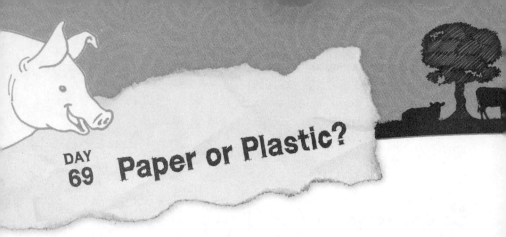

Paper or Plastic?

"We have here only five loaves of bread
and two fish," they answered.
"Bring them here to me," [Jesus] said.
MATTHEW 14:17-18, NIV

AT THE GROCERY STORE, the bagger often asks this question: "Paper or plastic?" So which is better for the environment? Well, both have advantages and downsides. The world produces 500 billion plastic bags every year. It can take up to a thousand years in a landfill for each bag to rot back into dirt. Also, plastic bags are often mistaken for food by marine wildlife such as whales, dolphins, and turtles. When eaten, the plastic can make animals sick or even kill them.

The best thing to do with plastic bags is reuse or refuse. Either reuse bags by saving them and bringing them when you shop the next time, or skip the plastic and ask for paper bags instead. Paper bags turn back into soil in months or a few years, and they can also be reused. The problem with paper bags is that they take 40 percent more energy to produce than plastic bags do, and the production of paper bags causes more air pollution too. Every year, 14 million trees are made into 10 billion paper sacks in the United States.

The solution? Reuse! Recycle! Both paper and plastic bags can be reused, so remember to bring used ones when you shop. But the best solution is to use canvas shopping bags. Many supermarkets give refunds to shoppers who bring their own bags, so bring your own!

 ## Connection

In Matthew 14, we see the story of how the disciples brought five loaves of bread and two fish to Jesus. Jesus took the food and multiplied it so there was enough for 5,000 people—with leftovers! It might seem a small thing to bring your own bag to the store each time, but God makes big things out of small ones. You can help a lot by doing just a little.

 ## What Can I Do?

Refuse *shopping bags.* If the bagger asks, "Paper or plastic?" just say, "No, thanks!" Maybe you can offer to be the person in your family who collects canvas bags around the house that can be used for shopping, or the one who makes sure the bags are in the car before each trip to the store. If you're just buying one or two things, you don't need a bag at all!

 ## A Trashy Experiment

Daniel Burd, a Canadian teenager, buried some plastic bags in dirt from a landfill. The dirt was crawling with bacteria that break down plastic into microscopic pieces. Daniel added salt and yeast to help the bacteria grow. In just four weeks, the bacteria had broken down one-fifth of the plastic. Scientists may use bacteria like this in landfills to lessen the damage that plastic bags do.

Factoid

Organizers made giant banners for the Democratic national convention held in Denver in 2008. Now a creative nonprofit organization has turned those colorful red, white, and blue banners into nonpolitical designer shopping bags. It's recycling for reuse!

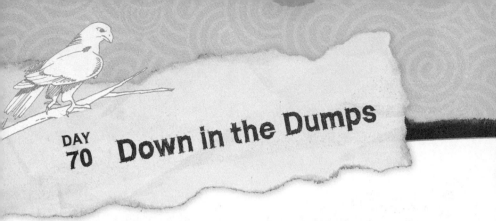

Down in the Dumps

Be careful to follow all the commands of the LORD your God, that you may possess this good land and pass it on as an inheritance to your descendants forever.
1 CHRONICLES 28:8, NIV

WE CAN'T RECYCLE or reuse everything (yet!). So a lot of our waste goes into landfills. Since before recorded history, people have used trash pits to throw away their waste. In the past, these pits gave off a horrible odor and attracted disease-carrying mosquitoes, flies, and rats. Ick. Even in modern times, garbage dumps can be dangerous. Sometimes hazardous waste in landfills (from things like batteries, paint, and bug poison) has leaked into the drinking water supply. Once scientists figured out what was happening, the government made rules for where garbage can end up. Landfills can only be built where there is rock or clay at the foundation to contain the trash. The sides of landfills need to be lined with heavy plastic or clay to keep the waste from poisoning the soil and water around it. Wells are drilled regularly to check the water nearby to be sure it's not being contaminated.

When a landfill is full, it's covered with dirt and planted with grass seed to blend back into the landscape. Landfills can also be made into parks or golf courses so they aren't eyesores on the landscape. It's not a good idea to build houses on them, though, because the landfill ground takes many years to settle. Trash needs air and water to decompose back into dirt. Our modern, carefully sealed trash dumps keep us safe from the waste, but they mummify the trash. To solve this problem, engineers are designing something called bioreactor landfills, which pump air and water into landfills to help the trash degrade. Another new landfill design includes a power station that burns the methane from the landfill for energy.

Connection

Scientists discovered that trash doesn't turn back into good soil if it is buried and sealed up from air and water. It's not a good idea to keep our problems sealed inside us, either. We need to expose them to the fresh air and living water of the Holy Spirit to get rid of them. The Bible says, "If we confess our sins to [God], he is faithful and just to forgive us our sins and to cleanse us from all wickedness" (1 John 1:9). If you have a problem, talk to God and to others. Admit your mistakes, and ask God to make you clean again.

What Can I Do?

Reduce your trash output. Ask your parents to let you do an experiment: get a trash can and put all your own trash in it for a week. How much is there? Can you think of ways to create less trash?

Factoid

In the United States today, we still dump 55 percent of our waste into landfills. The rest is recycled or burned.

Stinky Fact

Methane gas comes from rotting garbage, but we also use it to heat our homes. It is actually odorless (it loses the garbage smell after it is converted into a gas). The gas companies add a nasty "rotten egg" odor to it to warn people of gas leaks.

DAY 71 Clean and Natural

Work willingly at whatever you do,
as though you were working for the Lord
rather than for people.
COLOSSIANS 3:23

WE ALL *LOVE* to clean house, right? Well, maybe not. But if you've done any cleaning, you've probably noticed that lots of cleaning products have harsh, irritating chemicals that make your nose run and your eyes water when you use them. For example, many cleaners contain chlorine, which kills bacteria, algae, and fish. That's great for sinks and swimming pools, but it damages rivers and lakes.

Using natural cleaning products that don't have toxic (poisonous) ingredients prevents air and water pollution and saves you money. Besides that, it just might save you a sneeze or two! (See the next page for some ideas.)

 Connection

Colossians 3:23 reminds us that no matter what we're doing—
even if it's chores around the house—we're really doing it for God.
The next time you find yourself cleaning, think about how you
might do that the best you can—with both your attitude and the
cleaning supplies you use. It pleases God when we take good care
of ourselves, spend our money wisely, and take care of his world.
Galatians 6:5 says, "We are each responsible for our own conduct."

What Can I Do?

Rethink *the way you clean.* People can easily make their own
natural household cleaners for *one-tenth* of the cost of buying
commercial cleaners. Plus, they are better for you and better for
God's world. Become a "mad scientist" by mixing up some "Garden
of Eden" cleaners for you and your family. Hey, that will mean more
money for fun things . . . like ice cream! Here are some things you
can make:

- *Sink and tub scrubber:* In a bowl, mix ½ cup of baking soda
  and enough liquid detergent to make a texture like pudding.
  Scoop the goop onto a sponge, and then scrub the tub, sink, and
  shower. Just mix up as much as you need each time you clean
  the bathroom.
- *All-purpose spray cleaner:* Take ½ teaspoon of Arm & Hammer
  Super Washing Soda *or* ½ teaspoon of 20 Mule Team Borax, a
  couple of drops of liquid hand soap, and 2 cups of hot tap water.
  Pour these ingredients into a spray bottle. (You can reuse an
  old spray bottle to reduce plastic waste.) Screw on the top of the
  spray bottle firmly and shake until the washing soda has dis-
  solved. Use it to clean just about everything.

May their land be blessed by the LORD with the precious gift
of dew from the heavens and water from beneath the earth.
DEUTERONOMY 33:13

HOW MUCH WATER do you think the average American family uses each day by flushing their toilets? Believe it or not, the answer is 50 gallons. That's as much as 190 one-liter pop bottles!

Each year there are more and more people on this Earth, and they all need water. Even though there's a lot of water on our planet, most of it is seawater—about 97 percent. Another 2 percent is ice at the North and South Poles. Of all the water on land, only a tiny fraction is pure enough to drink. Some water has pollution, sewage, or microbes in it that can make humans very sick. Only about one-tenth of one percent of the Earth's water is available for us to drink. No wonder it is considered such a precious resource to save!

 Connection

Water is a gift from God. It's up to us to manage it wisely. In Matthew 24:45, Jesus says, "A faithful, sensible servant is one to whom the master can give . . . responsibility." Here are three ways you and your family can be good "water stewards" each day:

 What Can I Do? *Reduce.*

- **Check your toilet for leaks.** Take the lid off your toilet and pour some food coloring into the tank. Set a timer for 30 minutes, then go back and check the toilet bowl. If the bowl water is colored,

that means the toilet is leaking and it's wasting many
gallons of water each day. Ask your parents if they can
relace the valve.

- **Make your own low-flow toilet.** You can make your own low-
  flow toilet in about two minutes. Just fill a liter bottle with water
  and put it in the corner of your toilet tank farthest from the
  float. Now every time you flush, you're saving a liter of water.
  Plus, you're reusing a plastic bottle at the same time. Way to go!
- **Think before you flush.** Talk to your family about adopting the
  motto "Let the yellow mellow!" If you only flush once or twice a
  day, you are saving lots of water.

Let's Play with Water!

You will need a large tank, a graduated pitcher or measuring cup
that can hold 500 ml, an eye dropper, and some water.

1. Fill an aquarium with 20 liters of water. Pretend it's Earth's water.

2. Now, remove 500 ml of water and put it in the pitcher or
   measuring cup. What is left in the tank represents the amount
   of saltwater in all the oceans and seas of the world.

3. Take your pitcher and pour out 375 ml. This represents the
   amount of water in the ice caps (the Arctic and Antarctica).

4. You should have about 125 ml left. Take out five drops. This represents the water that is too far underground for us to get to.

5. The amount of water you have left in your pitcher represents the
   amount of fresh water we have to drink in the world!

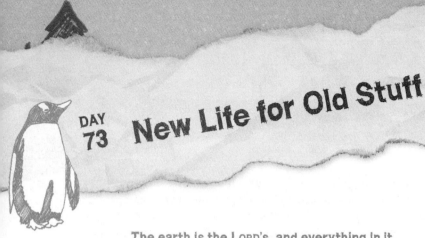

New Life for Old Stuff

The earth is the LORD's, and everything in it.
1 CORINTHIANS 10:26

THINK ABOUT the thing you have that you value most. Maybe it's something you saved up for a long time to buy, or maybe it's a collection you've been adding to for many years. Some people care a lot about their music, video games, clothes, or sports equipment. But did you know that nothing you have really belongs to you? That's because everything in this whole world—including all your stuff—actually belongs to God. He made everything and owns everything, and he has just loaned these things to us temporarily. He expects us to take care of them while we're here on Earth. One of the ways we can take care of the things we've been given is by coming up with creative ideas for reusing them.

Joke

A girl decided to help her family trim their budget, so instead of having her outfit dry-cleaned, she washed it by hand. Proud of her savings, she boasted to her dad, "Just think, we're five dollars richer because I washed this dress by hand."

"Good," her dad quickly replied. "Wash it again!"

Connection

We can give new purpose to things that otherwise would be thrown away. When we do this, it's like what God does for us. He doesn't leave us in our worn-down state; he gives us new life and a second chance: "Though outwardly we are wasting away, yet inwardly we are being renewed day by day" (2 Corinthians 4:16, NIV).

What Can I Do?

Reuse your kitchen stuff. There are dozens of creative ways to reuse things in the kitchen. Fold up empty butter wrappers and put them in the door of the refrigerator, then use them later to grease pans. Use egg cartons to store craft items, small LEGO pieces, Christmas decorations, or screws and nails. (Even better, you can buy eggs in cardboard egg cartons, since they can be recycled.)

Reuse your clothing. Swap clothes with a friend, and get "new to you" stuff to wear. Really old clothes can be used for rags. You can also shop at secondhand stores or garage sales. You might even take a challenge not to buy any new clothes for six months or a year.

Read and return. Number one on the amazingly reused list is library books. Before you go out and buy books, movies, music, or audiobooks, see if your local library has the title you're looking for. Many items are checked out over 100 times before they are sent off to be recycled. Now that's what you call reuse!

Review ideas together. Ask your parents if you can tape a piece of notebook paper (reused, of course) on the refrigerator door. Family members can write down ideas they come up with for reusing things around the house and community.

Use it up, wear it out, make it do . . . or do without!

David got up from the ground, washed himself,
put on lotions, and changed his clothes.
He went to the Tabernacle and worshiped the LORD.
2 SAMUEL 12:20

THE NUMBER ONE water user in your house is the toilet. Showers and baths are number two. Here's a quick experiment to find out how much water you use showering. You'll need a plastic ruler and a timer. Set the timer for 10 minutes, plug the tub drain, hop in, and take a 10-minute shower. Then measure the water in the tub. Is there an inch? more? The next time you shower, plug the tub drain again, and set the timer for four minutes this time. Measure the water after your shower. How many inches are there? How many gallons of water do you think you saved by taking a four-minute shower? (Hint: each inch of water in a standard bathtub equals about four and a half gallons of water.)

The clothes dryer is one of the biggest electric energy gobblers in your house. The energy used to dry one load of clothes costs at least 50 cents. How many loads of clothes does your family dry each week? Seven loads would cost $3.50 a week. Multiply that by 52 weeks in the year. How much does your clothes drying cost per year?

Riddle

Q: What gets wetter the more it dries?
A: A towel.

Connection

Jesus had something to say about another kind of energy too—the energy inside of us. We often put a lot of effort into things that don't matter too much in the long run, but he wants us to focus on what's really important: "Spend your energy seeking the eternal life that the Son of Man can give you" (John 6:27).

 What Can I Do?

Rethink your laundry. Ask your parents if you can make a solar clothes dryer. It will only cost you about five dollars! You will need:

- A 20-foot length of clothesline, tied to a tree or porch
- Clothespins
- Sunshine

If you don't have a backyard or if it's too cold outside, try setting up the clothesline in a basement or a garage.

CAROLINE SAYS

When I was growing up, my family didn't have a dryer. We hung our clothes outside, even in the winter. The laundry would "freeze-dry"! Now I have a dryer, but I still try to save energy. Whenever I can, I hang our washing on the line. I also have a folding clothes rack I set outside. It's handy—and if it starts to rain, we can just pick up the rack and bring it indoors.

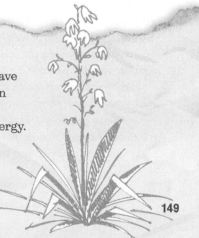

The Dark Side of Paper

DAY 75

In the house of the wise are stores of choice food and oil,
but a foolish man devours all he has.
PROVERBS 21:20, NIV

PAPER IS PRETTY amazing stuff. You can write on it, paint on it, make it into hats or paper airplanes, and use it to wipe things up. There's notebook paper, newspaper, sandpaper, litmus paper, blotting paper, wrapping paper, and even—you guessed it— toilet paper! You can use paper to cover Christmas presents and mail packages. There are even clothes, tablecloths, tea bags, and underground water pipes made of paper.

But there is a dark side to paper too. For one thing, it's made from trees. Each year Americans use 9 million trees' worth of receipts from stores, ATMs, and gas stations. And the loss of trees isn't the only problem. When tree wood is ground up, it's soaked in chlorine, sulfur dioxide, and other chemicals to make it white. The papermaking process produces dioxins, which are poisonous to plants and animals.

Even though a lot of things that used to require paper can now be done using computers and other technology, we still need paper for many purposes. But what many people don't realize is that some kinds of paper are better than others. Take a look at the suggestions on the next page to see how you can choose your paper wisely.

♻️ Connection

Paper has two sides (and we don't mean the front and the back). The good side of paper is that it can be used for lots of great things. The bad side is that it can cause pollution and clog landfills. God wants us to be careful of how we use our resources. As Proverbs 21:20 says, that's the way wise people handle things—they're careful with what they have today so they'll have enough tomorrow too.

What Can I Do?

Rethink your paper.

- Ask your parents if you can buy recycled or unbleached paper products. Unbleached papers are less harmful to the environment, because not as many chemicals are required to make them. You can find them in most stores.
- Use both sides of your paper when doing homework.
- Cut up used paper to make scratch paper.
- Save used printer paper and use the blank side when printing out documents on your computer.
- Ask your parents if your family can use cloth napkins for meals. Each person could have his or her own color or pattern. The napkins can be washed once a week or so (more often if you have barbecue!).

☀️ Factoid

Americans in restaurants and homes use an average of six paper napkins per person per day. If everyone used one less paper napkin a day, Americans would save 300 million napkins daily. That would save about 3,400 trees!

DAY 76 Energy Vampires

The prudent carefully consider their steps.
PROVERBS 14:15

WHAT HAS A little red light and sucks up energy? An electronic appliance left on standby mode. When TVs, DVD players, and cable boxes are in standby mode, they use almost half as much energy as they do when they are running. This also goes for computers left in sleep mode. When printers are left on, they use a lot of energy too.

What has a little green light and sucks up energy? A charger. Cell phone chargers draw electricity when they are plugged in, even if your phone isn't plugged into them. The same is true for chargers for laptops, digital cameras, BlackBerrys, and MP3 players and iPods.

Joke

Boy: "My dog likes to sit down each evening and surf the Net."

Girl: "What a smart animal!"

Boy: "Not really. It took the cat three weeks to teach him."

Connection

It's fun to think about ordinary things in a new way. You've seen little red and green lights on the electronics in your house for years, but maybe until now you didn't think about what they mean. In the same way, God shows us new things every day—things we never thought about in that way before. In Isaiah 48:6, God tells the Israelites, "Now I will tell you new things, secrets you have not yet heard." Pay attention—he just might be telling you something new too!

What Can I Do?

Reduce your energy. Stand by to save money: unplug those chargers! Your family could save up to $100 a year on your energy bill by doing this. Also, you can plug your other electronics into a power strip and turn off the strip when you're not using them. Remember: no more sleep mode, no more standby mode—these are energy vampires. You can also be an "energy monitor." Go around the house turning off the lights in empty rooms.

Rethink your lights. Ask your parents if your family can start using compact fluorescent lightbulbs. These spiral-shaped bulbs cost a little more to buy, but they end up saving money and energy because they are more efficient and last longer than regular bulbs.

Fun Fact

A laptop uses one-third of the energy of a full-size computer.

Caring for Our Pets

The godly care for their animals.
PROVERBS 12:10

DO YOU HAVE A PET? In the United States, dogs and cats are the most popular pets. Did you know that pets are good for your health? Studies show that elderly people who have pets tend to live longer—probably because they have something to love and take care of.

Pets are fun, but they are also a lot of work. Buying a pet means you promise to feed it, exercise it, give it lots of time and love, and take care of its health for its whole life. Millions of pets are sent to pounds each year after their owners realize the animals are more work than they bargained for.

Most pets make great companions. They love you and want to spend time with you even on your worst day. It's wise to think twice before getting an exotic pet though. These animals are often taken from the wild and shipped to pet stores. They don't do well in captivity, and often they don't bond with people.

Fun Facts
Top Five U.S. Pets

#1: fish
#2: cats
#3: dogs
#4: small animals (gerbils, hamsters, guinea pigs, rabbits)
#5: birds

Connection

God has given us responsibility for taking care of his animals. He also gave us the ability to tame some of them, as well as the blessing of their companionship. He is pleased when we feed them, exercise them, and give them lots of love. And for your pet, love is spelled T-I-M-E. When you take care of your pet, you can think of the verse in Proverbs and remember that it's a sign of godliness to treat animals well.

🚶 What Can I Do?

Readopt *a pet.* There are hundreds of thousands of "pre-owned" pets in animal shelters. The next time you get a pet, consider picking one up from a shelter. Give that pet a second chance at a happy life with a loving family. (And if you have a cat, how about trying Yesterday's News, a cat litter made from recycled paper?)

Retrace *your pet's steps.* Take advantage of the newest technology. Your vet can implant a microchip under the skin on your pet's front leg. This chip contains your name and address. If the pet gets lost and is taken to an animal shelter, the chip can be scanned and you'll be called and told that your pet has been found.

CAROLINE SAYS

I learned a lot about God from my dog. My dog loved me faithfully and constantly. He trusted me completely. That's how I want to learn to love God.

155

Have a Green Christmas

> If you have a gift for showing kindness
> to others, do it gladly.
> **ROMANS 12:8**

CHRISTMAS IS SUPPOSED to be one of the most wonderful times of the year . . . but it can also be one of the worst times of the year for the environment. Here are some facts you should know about what happens to our Earth every December:

- Each year, 1.9 billion holiday cards are sent in the United States. All those cards require 300,000 new trees to be cut down yearly.
- All the shopping bags, food waste, packaging, wrapping paper, and accessories used in December add up to one million more tons a week being added to landfills—25 percent more landfill waste than in any other month.

By now you may be wondering if this is the best way to celebrate Christmas. But taking care of the Earth doesn't have to mean giving up fun traditions altogether. With a little planning and creativity, you can have a holiday season that is even more meaningful for your family—and friendly to the world God made.

 Connection

Take another look at the verse from Romans above and remember that some gifts can't be wrapped—things like loving others and showing kindness. Jesus told us that we should really treasure him, not our stuff: "Sell your possessions and give to those in need. This will store up treasure for you in heaven! . . . Wherever your treasure is, there the desires of your heart will also be" (Luke 12:33-34).

156

 ## What Can I Do?

Rethink *gift giving.* Instead of buying stuff for your friends and family, consider giving them punch cards for services or favors. Another idea is to find organizations that allow you to buy and donate animals, such as goats and cows, to struggling families in developing countries around the world. Go to http://www.worldvision.org or http://www.foodforthepoor.org for more information.

Reuse *and rewrap.* Instead of throwing away those pesky packing peanuts, give your local mailing-supply store a call to see if they can reuse them. You can also make your own gift tags and thank-you notes by cutting up old cards or using scrap paper and stickers.

Factoid

If every family in the country gift wrapped just three gifts using paper they already have, the paper saved would be enough to cover 45,000 football fields.

Caroline Says

When I was a little girl, my mom drove me crazy by insisting that we not rip open our packages. Instead, we had to carefully cut the tape and save the paper for another time. She had us do the same with ribbons and bows. One day my parents proudly announced that our family hadn't bought new wrapping paper for five years. I rolled my eyes. Back then it was not considered cool to save paper and bows. Fast-forward a few years, and guess what? Now I have a family of my own, and we save gift paper and bows just like my parents did! Whenever we can, we put gifts in those cool gift bags, which can be reused many times.

DAY 79
A Match Made in Heaven

God said, "Let the land produce vegetation:
seed-bearing plants and trees
on the land that bear fruit with seed in it,
according to their various kinds."
GENESIS 1:11, NIV

ISN'T THERE JUST something about green, growing things that makes us happy? God uses the image of trees and plants in the Bible to remind us about new life, hope, and his goodness to us. Our world needs new oxygen every day. God gives us this new fresh air by filling our world with lots of trees and plants that take in carbon dioxide gas and put out oxygen (see day #14).

Did you know there's something you can do to bring fresh air into your room? It's easy—all you have to do is add some plants. Plants also get rid of icky odors and make your room smell better. (This will probably make your parents happy too.)

 Connection

Plants can bring freshness into the air, but God is the one we can thank for giving us each breath. Acts 17:25 says, "He himself gives life and breath to everything, and he satisfies every need."

 **What Can I Do?**

Replant. Here is a fun, cheap idea for freshening up any room in your house: buy a plant. Even better, ask for a cutting from someone else's houseplant. "Plant people" love to share. Just snip off a section of the plant with several leaves on it, making your cut near the main branch of the plant so there is plenty of stem on the cutting. Put the cutting on your windowsill in a (reused) glass jar of water. Once some good long roots grow (in about two or three weeks), it'll be ready to plant. Then you can plant the cutting in a small pot, using potting soil or dirt from your yard. You can also grow plants from single-leaf cuttings, although that takes a little longer. Some house-plants that work well for cuttings are jade plants, begonias, wandering Jew, vinca, and pothos.

Refresh others. You can give the gift of fresh air in the form of plants for birthdays or Christmas. Decorate the pots with stickers, ribbons, or acrylic paint if you want to. (Tip from Caroline, who found out the hard way: decorate the pots *before* you put the plants in them!)

 Fun Quote

"I have a rock garden. Last week three of them died."
—RICHARD DIRAN

DAY 80
Broccoli and Tea Bags

God said, "I give you every seed-bearing
plant on the face of the whole earth and every tree that has
fruit with seed in it. They will be yours for food."
GENESIS 1:29, NIV

HAVE YOU EVER seen a compost pile before? It's made from food scraps and plant waste that are mixed together and left to break down into natural fertilizer. Compost can be mixed in with the dirt in gardens to help grow big, healthy plants. Composting isn't a new idea—it has been going on for thousands of years. When some Native American groups planted corn, they buried fish heads in the holes along with the seeds, to fertilize the soil.

Joke

Q: What do you call a vegetable that you can use to brush your teeth?

A: Bristle sprouts.

♻ Connection

After Jesus miraculously fed the group of 5,000, he told his disciples, "Now gather the leftovers, so that nothing is wasted" (John 6:12). Food is one of the daily gifts God gives us. Let's not waste it.

 What Can I Do?

Recycle your food. You can make your very own recycling center in your own backyard. With your parents' permission, you can create a compost pile in an unused corner of the yard. Some people make a round compost corral (about four feet by four feet) out of chicken wire to contain the compost and keep it from blowing away. Here's how to make a compost pile: (1) Mix together dried leaves and dirt—your pile should be about the size of a laundry basket. (2) Add food scraps such as fruit and vegetable peelings, eggshells, and coffee grounds. (3) The pile should have equal amounts of inside stuff (household food scraps) and outside stuff: leaves, old potting soil, shredded newspaper, and grass clippings. (4) Stir up the pile once a week with a shovel or pitchfork. (5) Add water to the pile every few days if you live where there isn't much rain. Once the compost is nice and dark and crumbly, you can mix it in with your garden dirt. You'll never have to buy store fertilizer again.

CAROLINE SAYS

When I was a little girl, my mom had a covered wooden bucket, lined with plastic, on the kitchen counter by the sink. My family put all our leftover food in it (except meat): eggshells, coffee grounds, vegetable peelings, apple cores, broccoli, and tea bags. When the bucket got full, Mom would take it out to the corner of her big vegetable garden and dump it in her compost pile, along with our grass clippings.

More than You Need

In the morning . . . when the dew was gone,
thin flakes like frost on the ground appeared on the desert floor.
When the Israelites saw it, they said . . . "What is it?". . .
Moses said to them, "It is the bread the LORD has given you to eat.
This is what the LORD has commanded:
'Each one is to gather as much as he needs.'"
EXODUS 16:13-16, NIV

IT'S ALARMING how much food gets wasted each year in the
United States. Restaurants throw leftover food into their Dump-
sters. Grocery stores throw away fruit and vegetables that don't
sell. People throw their leftovers into the trash. Almost half of the
food grown in the United States gets wasted. All that food goes into
landfills, where it stinks and attracts flies.

There are many ways to improve this situation. Restaurants can
donate nonperishable items to food pantries. Many grocery stores
give their day-old bread to churches and nonprofit organizations
so it can be distributed to people in need. Individual families can
really cut down on wasted food by incorporating leftovers into new
meals and freezing leftovers. There are lots of great cookbooks to
use as resources. One is *The Use-It-Up Cookbook: Creative Recipes
for the Frugal Cook* by Catherine Kitcho.

Joke

Knock, knock. Who's there? Arthur. Arthur who?
Arthur any leftovers?

 Connection

God gave the Israelites quail (birds) and manna (a little like bread) to eat when they were hungry in the desert. Some of the people tried to take more than they needed. "They kept part of it until morning, but it was full of maggots and began to smell" (Exodus 16:20, NIV). God gives us just what we need for each day— there's no need to try to hoard more than that.

What Can I Do?

Reduce your food waste. The next time you put food on your plate, take only as much as you're sure you can eat. God wants us to be wise with everything he has given us . . . and not waste it.

Rethink your leftovers. There are lots of things you can do with leftover food. How about putting your apple cores in the backyard for the squirrels? Or maybe you can crumble up your bread crusts for the birds to eat. Get creative with your recipes and see how many of your leftovers you can fit into your next meal!

Three Things You Can Do with Leftover Christmas Fruitcake

1. Donate it to the school library for a bookend.
2. Stand on it to change a lightbulb.
3. Use it for a science project.

163

Solar Ovens

The Son radiates God's own glory and expresses the very character of God, and he sustains everything by the mighty power of his command.
HEBREWS 1:3

SOLAR OVENS ARE becoming the hot new thing. They are powered by the sun, not electricity. They are off the power grid, meaning you can use them without tapping into electrical power. That means they cost nothing to use. Solar ovens can take different forms, but basically they are self-contained boxes that are set outside in the sun. In general, it takes about twice as long to cook something in a solar oven as it does in a conventional oven. Solar ovens are great for baking potatoes and other vegetables, for melting cheese on crackers, and for making s'mores. They don't work well for baking bread or roasting meat, though, because they don't get hot enough and they don't maintain an even temperature.

Food baked in a solar oven will cook faster in the summer than in the winter. Do you have any guesses why that is?

Joke

Q: Why did the baked potato cross the road?

A: He saw a fork up ahead.

♻ Connection

The solar oven is a way to capture the power of the sun. In the same way, the Bible helps us focus on God and live in his strength. Reading God's Word and memorizing verses are wonderful ways to stay connected to our true Power Source (see Psalm 119:11).

What Can I Do?

Rethink your cooking methods. Build your own solar oven with:

- a cardboard pizza box
- a box cutter or scissors
- heavy plastic wrap
- tape (not duct tape)
- aluminum foil
- black construction paper
- a ruler

Trace a big square on the lid of the pizza box, one inch smaller than the lid. Cut three sides of the square, leaving the fourth side (at the back) uncut to make a flap. Open the box and cover the window you cut with plastic wrap. Seal the wrap with tape. Next, line the inside bottom and sides of the box with foil. Line the inside of the flap you cut with foil. Then cover the inside bottom of the box with black paper. Put the food (such as crackers with cheese) inside the oven. Close the box. Put the oven in direct sunlight. Angle the foil-covered flap so it catches the sun and reflects it into the oven. Prop the flap open at a right angle with your ruler. Tape it in place. Check the oven in 30 minutes to see if the cheese has melted. You can go to http://www.hometrainingtools.com/articles/build-a-solar-oven-project.html for more information about how to assemble your oven.

Heroes in Your Garden

The LORD God planted a garden in Eden.
GENESIS 2:8

DID YOU KNOW that one-third of the food on your table comes to you thanks to the hard work of pollinator insects and animals? Most plants are only able to make seeds (or reproduce) after they have been pollinated. Plants and pollinators work together to make new plants. They both get something out of the relationship. The pollinators get to eat, and when they move from plant to plant, they transfer pollen, which starts the process for a new plant to be formed.

Each pollinator insect or animal has its own favorite snacks. Bees are attracted to marigolds, daisies, mint, thyme, and lavender. Butterflies will flock to zinnias, yarrow, daisies, milkweed, violets, hollyhocks, and black-eyed Susans. Some favorites of pollinating beetles are asters, sunflowers, and roses. Hummingbirds love honeysuckle, sage, fuchsia, and nasturtiums. Bats of the Southwest like night-blooming flowers such as agave and cactus.

In our modern world full of high rises and parking lots, it's getting harder for pollinators to find the plants they need. But there's something you can do to help! You can plant pollinator-attracting plants and flowers in your own backyard.

♻ Connection

One of the first things God did after he created the first human was to plant a garden (see today's verse from Genesis). It's fascinating how God chose to make pollinators and plants work together to produce food. A world without pollinators would make our lives and our gardens less fruitful. Everything we learn about science and nature points to the fact that we have a wonderful and creative God.

What Can I Do?

Restore a piece of Eden. You can plant your very own pollinator garden. Even a few pots of flowers on your patio or deck will delight the pollinators in your neighborhood. It's a good idea to plant flowers and herbs that are native to your area, because they will make the best attractors for pollinators. Plant your flowers in a sunny location, and don't use pesticides on them. A great Web site to help you get started is http://www.kidsgardening.com.

Joke

Q: What kind of flowers would King Tut like best?

A: Chrysanthemummies.

Trees and Rivers: From Genesis to Revelation

DAY 84

> Blessed are those who wash their robes,
> that they may have the right to the tree of life.
> REVELATION 22:14, NIV

HAVE YOU EVER wondered what God thinks about trees? How about rivers? Believe it or not, both of these parts of nature play an important role in the story of his people. In fact, the Bible itself begins and ends with rivers and trees.

In the very beginning of the Bible story, Genesis describes humankind's first home in the Garden of Eden. It's by a river: "A river watering the garden flowed from Eden" (Genesis 2:10, NIV). Two great trees grew in the center of the Garden, called the "tree of life" and the "tree of the knowledge of good and evil" (Genesis 2:9).

In the book of Revelation, the last book of the Bible, we see that our forever home will be beside a river. In his vision of heaven, this is what the disciple John saw: "The angel showed me the river of the water of life, as clear as crystal, flowing from the throne of God . . . down the middle of the great street of the city" (Revelation 22:1-2, NIV). And if you think that sounds cool, the tree of all trees will also be there: "On each side of the river grew a tree of life. . . . The leaves were used for medicine to heal the nations" (Revelation 22:2).

Both the river and the tree bring life and healing. In Eden, Adam and Eve sinned and could no longer eat the life-giving fruit of the tree. In heaven, we will be able to eat that fruit of life again, thanks to the sacrifice that Jesus made for us.

♻ Connection

Only God can make it possible for us to drink from that heavenly river and eat from the tree of life described in Revelation 22. While we wait, he has given us rivers and trees to care for here on Earth. They can remind us of the even better rivers and trees in heaven. How does God make it possible for us to eat that amazing fruit and drink that superwater someday? He wants us to love and follow him. Is Jesus the center of your life?

 What Can I Do?

Refresh *your soul.* Spend time enjoying your local greenbelts and parks. We are designed to have contact with trees and birds and weeds and frogs! They remind us of their creator—and ours.

Renew *the land.* Plant a tree in your community! In most places, you can volunteer to plant saplings in state parks or add greenery in your neighborhood, but always make sure it is okay to do so first. You can find a good checklist at this site: http://www.na.fs.fed.us/Spfo/pubs/uf/plant_trees/planting_trees.htm.

Joke

Q: Why is the Mississippi such an unusual river?

A: It has four *i*'s, but it can't see.

Don't Forget to Mow the Roof

They are like plants in the field, like tender green shoots,
like grass sprouting on the roof.
2 KINGS 19:26, NIV

A MUSEUM IN San Francisco has really gone green: their roof is growing! The California Academy of Sciences in Golden Gate Park boasts the biggest plant-covered roof in California. The science museum's top is blanketed in 2 million pounds of soil, trees, plants, and rare flowers that grow on seven artificial "roof hills." Each hill has skylights to bring natural light into a man-made coral reef and tropical rain forest inside the museum. The natural covering saves the museum 35 percent on their heating and cooling energy costs.

It used to be that cities took away the land area where things could grow and put up tall buildings in their place. Cities and towns had small flower boxes and trees planted along roads, but parking lots and buildings spread out in great plains of concrete and steel. These days, however, architects who design buildings are thinking of new ways to make cities greener. Covering rooftops in flower fields is one cool way they are doing it.

♻ Connection

The kind of grass on the housetop described in 2 Kings isn't quite like what the science museum has in mind. But thinking about how God can bring life in the most unlikely places—even on rooftops—reminds us of how alive and green God's world really is. Every inch of our natural world is covered with living things. Grasses, wildflowers, and trees grow in all kinds of places, wherever life can take hold. God is all about life and beauty.

What Can I Do?

Rethink *your air-conditioning.* God has designed living plants and trees to be air conditioners and natural coolers. Just as the roof in Golden Gate Park cools the museum, you can use a tree to cool your home! If there is an area on your house that gets lots of sunlight in the summer, ask your parents if you can plant a tree to cast shade on it. In the fall, the tree will drop its leaves so that the winter sun can still warm your house when you need it most.

Jokes

Q: What do trees drink?
A: Root beer.

Q: What happened to the plant in math class?
A: It grew square roots.

Q: Why is grass so dangerous?
A: Because it's full of blades.

A Bed-and-Breakfast Goes Green

If any of you lacks wisdom, he should ask God, who gives generously to all without finding fault, and it will be given to him.
JAMES 1:5, NIV

WHEN GARY HARDIN opened his Briar Rose bed-and-breakfast a few years ago, he wanted to make it environmentally green. He explained why: "If you have a pet, you have to take care of it. If you don't, it won't be happy and healthy. The whole planet is really like that. Our just being here [on Earth] has a certain impact on the planet. What I can do is to work toward doing things that are *least* harmful."

Gary set about to do this in ways that we can all learn from. He replaced an old gas-guzzling furnace with a more efficient one, and he replaced carpets with recycled fiber rugs. The Briar Rose serves all organic food (food raised without pesticides or harmful chemical fertilizers). Instead of bottled water, the bed-and-breakfast serves filtered water in glass bottles with rubber stoppers. Guests can refill them with filtered water from the kitchen. "We use nontoxic cleaning products, and we've gotten rid of all the little soaps and shampoo bottles," Gary says. "Instead, we have natural organic shampoos and soaps in bottles, and we refill them. It was so frustrating to see little soap bars that would get used twice and then the whole thing's still there but you have to throw it away." Gary also plans to install photovoltaic panels, which turn sunlight into electricity and use less power from the city.

 Connection

God is pleased when we use the creative minds he has given us to guard his world and the creatures in it. As it says in the verse above, he will give us wisdom if we ask him for it.

 What Can I Do?

Request smart travel arrangements. Ask your parents if your family can stay at a "green" hotel next time you travel. You can encourage them to do the same if they travel for business. You'll find a list of environmentally friendly hotels at http://www.greenhotels.com.

Riddle

Q: What type of fruit has babies in a red house, a red house in a white house, and a white house in a green house?

A: A watermelon.

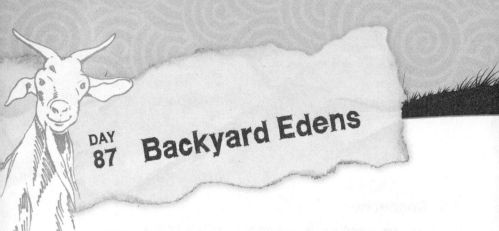

Backyard Edens

I [King Solomon] made gardens and parks, filling them
with all kinds of fruit trees. I built reservoirs to collect the
water to irrigate my many flourishing groves.
ECCLESIASTES 2:5-6

WALK AROUND YOUR neighborhood on a Saturday morning.
Listen to all those lawn mowers and Weedwackers. Look at
all those neighbors working on landscaping—planting and pruning
their yards to perfection. In countries all around the world, people
who have extra time and money often spend it on gardening. They
fertilize and mow their lawns, plant and prune shrubs and trees,
and grow flowers. They build fountains and fishponds. They buy
birdbaths and bird feeders to attract God's creatures to their
backyards.

This is nothing new. Even back in Bible times, wealthy people
spent time and money creating beautiful gardens—not to produce
food, but to create places to enjoy and relax in. Ancient Egyptians
planted ornamental gardens as early as 1500 BC. In 600 BC, King
Nebuchadnezzar II of Babylon built the Hanging Gardens of
Babylon, one of the seven wonders of the ancient world. The story
goes that he built them for his wife, Amytis of Media, who missed
the plants and trees of her homeland. The Hanging Gardens were
constructed of mud-brick terraces, one on top of the other, and they
were 350 feet tall. The terraces bloomed with every kind of plant,
tree, and flower that could be found. Beautiful lawns grew among
pools, fountains, and miniature waterfalls. The Gardens were built
near the Euphrates River, and a big pump carried river water up
the terraces to water the gardens. People still enjoy gardens of
many types and sizes all these years later.

 Connection

In Ecclesiastes, King Solomon described his efforts to make beautiful gardens and parks. Today, people still love to landscape and plant gardens. Have you ever wondered why? Maybe it is because there is a longing in us to recreate a little slice of Eden that was lost long ago. We put a lot of time into our backyards in an effort to create a peaceful, quiet, secluded place where we can enjoy trees and plants, watch birds, play with our pets, and maybe get a little closer to God.

 What Can I Do?

Reflect on a historical garden. Go to http://en.wikipedia.org/wiki/File:Pond_in_a_garden.jpg to see an image of an ancient Egyptian tomb painting. This painting is from around 1500 BC, and it shows a beautiful lotus pond surrounded by straight rows of palm and acacia trees. The way everything is evenly spaced out and organized shows that it was a human-made garden.

A-MAZE-ing Fact

The world's largest permanent hedge maze is the Pineapple Garden Maze at the Dole Plantation at Wahiawa, Hawaii. It is made up of 11,400 colorful Hawaiian plants.

Those who hope in the LORD
will renew their strength.
They will soar on wings like eagles.
ISAIAH 40:31, NIV

TAKE A LOOK AROUND your room. How many toys or devices do you have that run on batteries? Do you have an MP3 player? Got a cell phone or laptop in your house? Batteries are everywhere! If there are so many just in your house, imagine how many there are in the entire world! In the United States alone, people throw away 2 billion batteries every year. That pile of batteries is as heavy as about 320 midsize SUVs.

Here's the problem: batteries are made of heavy metals and acids that can leak into the ground. The nasty battery juice ends up poisoning wildlife and dribbling into our water. But there is an alternative: we can get rechargeable batteries. Rechargeable batteries are more expensive than regular ones, but they can be plugged into the wall and filled up with electricity again. You can reuse a rechargeable battery thousands of times.

 Connection

Do you ever feel like a run-down battery? When the Israelites—the people of God—were tired, the prophet Isaiah spoke God's words of encouragement to them. "Even youths will become weak and tired," he said. "But those who trust in the LORD will find new strength" (Isaiah 40:30-31). God's Spirit can be like a battery recharger for you. When you are feeling sad or tired, God can give you strength again. Talk things over with him and read his Word, and you will find new energy!

 What Can I Do?

Reuse and reduce. First, make a list of everything in your house that uses batteries. You might be surprised at how many batteries you are using. Figure out how you can use less—is there anything you can do without? Second, ask your parents if you can get a battery charger to cut back on battery waste.

 **Fun Fact**

The world's largest battery is in Fairbanks, Alaska. It is 21,500 square feet in size. In times of an electrical failure, it can power the homes of 12,000 people for up to seven minutes.

You Can Change the World!

Be glad; rejoice forever in my creation!
ISAIAH 65:18

JESUS CHANGED THE WORLD, one person at a time. Sure, sometimes he spoke to huge crowds. But he spent most of his time with his disciples: one-on-one, teacher to student, friend to friend. He was always a perfect model of who God wanted him to be. Everywhere he went, people wanted to be like him. He led by example and inspired those around him.

Here are a few young eco-heroes who have been in the news lately. A 15-year-old boy in Massachusetts created a high school food garden. The organic produce from the garden was used for school lunches and also donated to low-income families, and 1,000 pounds of food was donated in all. A 12-year-old boy in Abu Dhabi, United Arab Emirates, started a "Save the Camels" campaign to make people aware that many camels die each year because of trash in the desert. An eight-year-old boy in Maryland wrote and illustrated a book about butterflies. He sold copies of the book and donated the money to the World Wildlife Fund. Each of these kids received an award from the Action for Nature organization, which sponsors a yearly international contest spotlighting people who are working to help our environment. The cool things these kids have done to help care for the Earth can inspire the rest of us.

♻ Connection

Love is not a passive feeling. It is an action! Love is what we do.
Isaiah tells us to be glad, to rejoice forever in God's creation. Our
response to this should be . . . action! We can thank God for the
amazing world he has made. We can do things that make his world
more healthy and beautiful. We can tell others that God is the one
who created the natural beauty around us.

 What Can I Do?

Reflect on little ways to make a difference. Caring for the Earth
sometimes seems like an impossible job. But by following Jesus'
example, we can do it, one person at a time, one project at a time.
Pick up that piece of trash on the side of the road. Clean up that
mess in the park. Recycle that cardboard box or plastic bag. And
always remember: don't lecture your family and friends about taking care of God's world. Encourage them instead. Treat them with
the same love and respect that Jesus has for them. Inspire them
with your example.

Cool Quote

"Appreciation needs to lead to stewardship. Stewardship takes us
beyond appreciation to restoration. . . . Beyond restoration, stewardship means serving. As we understand that God through creation is
in so many ways serving us, we grow to willingly
return this service with our own."

— CALVIN DEWITT

Good News about a Bridge

DAY 90

God has given us eternal life, and this life is in his Son.
He who has the Son has life.
1 JOHN 5:11-12, NIV

IN THIS BOOK you have been learning a lot about God and
his creation. Out of all the wonderful things he made on this
whole planet, did you know that you are one of his most precious
creations? He has known you since even before you were born!
That's not all: the majestic, powerful God who created the heavens
and the Earth, who crafted the cycles in our world and designed the
beautiful creatures—that God wants you to know him too! He wants
you to enjoy being friends with him now, and someday he wants you
to live with him forever in heaven.

There are four important things to know about this:

1. God loves you, and he wants you to have a full, joy-filled life.
   In John 10:10, Jesus says, "My purpose is to give them a rich and
   satisfying life."
2. This is the bad news: we are separated from God by our sin.
   It's as if there's a giant canyon spread between us and God.
   Everybody has sin inside him or her. The Bible tells us that
   "everyone has sinned; we all fall short of God's glorious standard"
   (Romans 3:23). Many people try to get to God by being good, saying the right prayers, or doing just the right things. Living a good
   life certainly pleases God, but we can never be perfect enough to
   get into heaven! We need someone to build a bridge across that
   canyon between us and God, and God himself took care of
   this problem.

3. The good news is that there is a bridge across the canyon—that bridge is Jesus. It says in 1 Peter 3:18 that Christ "suffered for our sins once for all time. He never sinned, but he died for sinners to bring you safely home to God." When Jesus died on the cross and then rose again, he paid the price of our sin so that we could cross that canyon and be with God every day—in this life and in heaven.

4. We can cross that bridge by putting our faith, our trust, in Jesus. When you walk across a bridge over a river, you are trusting that it will hold you up. If you trust in Jesus alone (without trusting in being good, going to church, or saying the right things), he changes you into a new person—a child of God—forever. The Bible says, "To all who believed him and accepted him, he gave the right to become children of God" (John 1:12).

God has made it possible for you to have a relationship with him and to know—for sure—that if you died today, you would be with him in heaven forever. But eternal life with God doesn't start when you die; it starts as soon as you invite Jesus to be in charge of your life! If you don't know Jesus in this way, why not talk to him today? Ask him into your life. Tell him you want to be a new person from now on—that you want his wisdom and strength to carry you through life.

Your journey with Jesus will be the best adventure you can imagine. Along the way, God will help you do all kinds of great things . . . like caring for his creation!

Top 10 Tips for Creation Care

RESPECT

1. Pick up one piece of trash every day.
2. Bring a little Eden to your neighborhood: set up a bird feeder in the winter; plant a garden or a tree; create a compost pile.

REDUCE

3. Save water by taking four-minute showers. Remember what saving water did for Mono Lake!
4. Instead of having your parents drive you, walk or bike to nearby places.
5. Reduce power use by turning off lights. Don't leave your computer or DVD player on standby or sleep mode. Remember those energy vampires.

REUSE

6. Instead of buying new bottled water, refill your water bottle.
7. Reuse shopping bags. Save plastic or paper bags, or buy canvas ones to bring home the groceries.

RECYCLE

8. Recycle metal, glass, paper, and plastic.

RETHINK

9. Give acts of service instead of stuff.
10. Look at God's creation in new and different ways. He has given us the task of taking care of his world—every bit of it. Can you do it? Will you? Living at peace with God's creation makes our lives richer and brings us closer to our Creator.

Acknowledgments

WE WOULD LIKE to thank Greg Johnson at WordServe Literary for sharing in our vision of this book and helping it come to fruition. Katara Patton and Stephanie Voiland and the editorial and design staff at Tyndale nurtured that vision, encouraged us to make it even better, and then made us look good! Our thanks to Arne and Harriet Truman and Mark and Kelsey Gilliland, who spent hours reading and giving us valuable suggestions. Also, to Professor Steven Bouma-Prediger of Hope College, and to Professor Ellen F. Davis of Duke Divinity School, for insights and inspiration, theologically, historically, and environmentally. A project like this only comes to pass when the Lord is in it. Our prayer is that our words have communicated the heart of God to our readers!

About the Authors

CAROLINE AND MICHAEL CARROLL have written a dozen children's books together on subjects ranging from dinosaurs to ancient cities of the Bible. They teach writing classes at a local community college. Michael teaches art to children and adults, and Caroline is a children's librarian. Putting science and kids together is their favorite thing ever! They have two grown children who live near them in Littleton, Colorado.